CREATING WEB PAGES
WITH HTML

Simplified

3RD EDITION

Visual

by Sherry Willard Kinkoph

WILEY

Wiley Publishing, Inc.

CREATING WEB PAGES WITH HTML SIMPLIFIED®, 3RD EDITION

Published by
Wiley Publishing, Inc.
111 River Street
Hoboken, NJ 07030-5774

Published simultaneously in Canada

Library of Congress Control Number: 2005937344

ISBN-13: 978-0-471-78647-4

ISBN-10: 0-471-78647-0

Manufactured in the United States of America

10 9 8 7 6 5 4 3 2 1

Trademark Acknowledgments

Contact Us

For general information on our other products and services please contact our Customer Care Department within the U.S. at (800) 762-2974, outside the U.S. at (317) 572-3993, or fax (317) 572-4002.

For technical support please visit www.wiley.com/techsupport.

Wiley Publishing, Inc.

Sales

Contact Wiley at (800) 762-2974 or fax (317) 572-4002.

Praise for Visual Books

"Like a lot of other people, I understand things best when I see them visually. Your books really make learning easy and life more fun."

John T. Frey (Cadillac, MI)

"I have quite a few of your Visual books and have been very pleased with all of them. I love the way the lessons are presented!"

Mary Jane Newman (Yorba Linda, CA)

"I just purchased my third Visual book (my first two are dog-eared now!), and, once again, your product has surpassed my expectations."

Tracey Moore (Memphis, TN)

"I am an avid fan of your Visual books. If I need to learn anything, I just buy one of your books and learn the topic it in no time. Wonders! I have even trained my friends to give me Visual books as gifts."

Illona Bergstrom (Aventura, FL)

"Thank you for making it so clear. I appreciate it. I will buy many more Visual books."

J.P. Sangdong (North York, Ontario, Canada)

"I have several books from the Visual series and have always found them to be valuable resources."

Stephen P. Miller (Ballston Spa, NY)

"Thank you for the wonderful books you produce. It wasn't until I was an adult that I discovered how I learn — visually. Nothing compares to Visual books. I love the simple layout. I can just grab a book and use it at my computer, lesson by lesson. And I understand the material! You really know the way I think and learn. Thanks so much!"

Stacey Han (Avondale, AZ)

"I absolutely admire your company's work. Your books are terrific. The format is perfect, especially for visual learners like me. Keep them coming!"

Frederick A. Taylor, Jr. (New Port Richey, FL)

"I have several of your Visual books and they are the best I have ever used."

Stanley Clark (Crawfordville, FL)

"I bought my first Visual book last month. Wow. Now I want to learn everything in this easy format!"

Tom Vial (New York, NY)

"Thank you, thank you, thank you...for making it so easy for me to break into this high-tech world. I now own four of your books. I recommend them to anyone who is a beginner like myself."

Gay O'Donnell (Calgary, Alberta, Canada)

"I write to extend my thanks and appreciation for your books. They are clear, easy to follow, and straight to the point. Keep up the good work! I bought several of your books and they are just right! No regrets! I will always buy your books because they are the best."

Seward Kollie (Dakar, Senegal)

"Compliments to the chef!! Your books are extraordinary! Or, simply put, extra-ordinary, meaning way above the rest! THANK YOU THANK YOU THANK YOU! I buy them for friends, family, and colleagues."

Christine J. Manfrin (Castle Rock, CO)

"What fantastic teaching books you have produced! Congratulations to you and your staff. You deserve the Nobel Prize in Education in the Software category. Thanks for helping me understand computers."

Bruno Tonon (Melbourne, Australia)

"Over time, I have bought a number of your 'Read Less - Learn More' books. For me, they are THE way to learn anything easily. I learn easiest using your method of teaching."

José A. Mazón (Cuba, NY)

"I am an avid purchaser and reader of the Visual series, and they are the greatest computer books I've seen. The Visual books are perfect for people like myself who enjoy the computer, but want to know how to use it more efficiently. Your books have definitely given me a greater understanding of my computer, and have taught me to use it more effectively. Thank you very much for the hard work, effort, and dedication that you put into this series."

Alex Diaz (Las Vegas, NV)

Credits

Project Editor
Tim Borek

Acquisitions Editor
Jody Lefevere

Product Development Supervisor
Courtney Allen

Copy Editor
Nancy Rappoport

Technical Editor
Allen Wyatt

Editorial Manager
Robyn Siesky

Screen Artist
Jill A. Proll

Illustrators
Steven Amory
Matthew Bell
Elizabeth Cardenas-Nelson
Kristin Corley
Ronda David-Burroughs
Cheryl Grubbs
Sean Johanessen
Jacob Mansfield
Rita Marley
Paul Schmitt III

Book Design
Kathie Rickard

Production Coordinator
Adrienne Martinez

Layout
Jennifer Heleine
Amanda Spagnuolo

Proofreader
Shannon Ramsey

Quality Control
David Faust
Joe Niesen

Indexer
WordCo Indexing Services

Manufacturing
Allan Conley
Linda Cook
Paul Gilchrist
Jennifer Guynn

Vice President and Executive Group Publisher
Richard Swadley

Vice President and Publisher
Barry Pruett

Director of Composition Services
Debbie Stailey

About the Author

Sherry Willard Kinkoph has written and edited over 70 books over the past 10 years covering a variety of computer topics ranging from hardware to software, from Microsoft Office programs to the Internet. Her recent titles include *Master VISUALLY eBay Business Kit*, *Teach Yourself VISUALLY Photoshop Elements 3.0*, and *Teach Yourself VISUALLY Office 2003*. Sherry's ongoing quest is to help users of all levels master the ever-changing computer technologies. No matter how many times they — the software manufacturers and hardware conglomerates — throw out a new version or upgrade, Sherry vows to be there to make sense of it all and help computer users get the most out of their machines.

Author's Acknowledgments

Special thanks go out to publisher Barry Pruett and to acquisitions editor Jody Lefevere for allowing me the opportunity to tackle this exciting project; to project editors Tim Borek and Maureen Spears for their dedication and patience in guiding this project from start to finish; to copy editor Nancy Rappoport, for ensuring that all the i's were dotted and t's were crossed; to technical editor Allen Wyatt for skillfully checking each step and offering valuable input along the way; and finally to the production team at Wiley for their able efforts in creating such a visual masterpiece.

Table of Contents

Adding Text

Formatting Text

Table of Contents

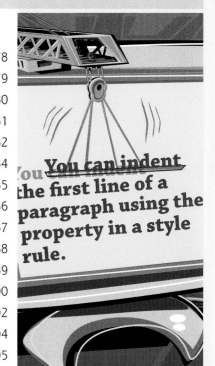

Adding Images

Adding Links

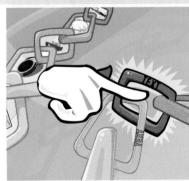

Table of Contents

Creating Forms

Adding Sounds and Videos

Table of Contents

Chapter 1

HTML and Web Page Basics

Are you interested in building your own Web pages? This chapter introduces you to basic HTML concepts and methods for creating your own Web content.

HTML

Internet Basics

The Internet has grown from a military research project in the late 1960s to a global network of computers today. The number of Internet users around the globe is expected to reach over 1 billion by the year 2005.

Offering everything from e-mail to information to commerce, the Internet brings users an unprecedented way to communicate and exchange data. Constructed of thousands of networks and computers around the world, the Internet connects organizations, governments, businesses, and individuals.

Types of Connections

Users connect to the Internet through a variety of sources. Individuals can connect through a modem and a phone line, cable, or satellite. If you use a modem to connect to the Internet, you typically utilize an *Internet service provider*, also called an ISP, or a commercial service, such as America Online. You can also use cable TV companies to connect to the Internet through a cable modem, or you can connect through digital phone lines, such as ISDN (Integrated Services Digital Network) and DSL (Digital Subscriber Line).

Connection Speeds

Connection speeds play an important part in a user's Internet experience. Slower connections result in slower file transfers and Web page viewing. Modem connections offer the slowest connection speeds to the Internet, up to 56 Kbps (Kilobits per second), followed by ISDN connections at 64–128 Kbps. Cable modems can achieve connection speeds up to 1.5 Mbps, while DSL offers speeds of 1,000–9,000 Kbps.

TCP/IP

Internet connection relies on a collection of protocols that govern how computers and networks talk to each other. *Transmission Control Protocol/Internet Protocol*, or TCP/IP for short, is simply a set of rules that control how information flows between computers and allows for individual computers to communicate with the Internet as if they are directly connected.

The World Wide Web

The World Wide Web is a giant collection of documents, or pages, stored on computers around the globe. Commonly called *the Web*, this collection of pages houses a wealth of text, images, audio, video, and more. Web pages are stored on *servers*, which are computers designed for holding and transferring data. When you place a document on a server, it is accessible for other users to view. Typically, companies, government agencies, organizations, and individuals maintain Web pages.

URLS and Links

Every page on the Web has a unique address, called a *URL*, short for Uniform Resource Locator. If you know a page's URL, you can view it over the Internet. You can also view pages using links. Hyperlinks, or *links*, connect pages through embedded URLs presented as text or images on a page. Users can jump from one page to another by clicking links. The activity of viewing Web pages is casually called *Web surfing*.

Browsers

To view Web pages, you must use a *Web browser*. Browsers are specialized programs that retrieve Web pages from servers and display them on a user's computer. Microsoft Internet Explorer and Netscape Navigator are the two most popular browsers used today. Other browsers are available, including Apple's Safari, Mozilla's Firefox, and Opera. Each program has evolved through a myriad of versions, each improving over the last. As you write HTML code, just remember that not all users have the most recent version of a particular browser.

An Introduction to HTML

Web pages are built using HTML, short for *HyperText Markup Language*. HTML documents are comprised of text and coding that instruct a Web browser how to display the data. HTML documents are identified by their .html or .htm file extension. Because any Web browser can read an HTML document, you do not need a special platform, such as Windows, UNIX, or Mac, to view the information.

HTML Coding

HTML coding consists of tags. Tags are individual instructions to the browser, and are surrounded by brackets, < >. Many tags include an opening tag and a closing tag. When writing tags, you can use upper or lowercase letters. To make the coding easy to read, most users type it in uppercase to distinguish the coding from regular text data on the page. Tags can also include attributes you can define, such as color values or measurements.

HTML Standards

The World Wide Web Consortium, or W3C for short, sets HTML standards. This international group consists of the Web's founders and industry leaders, including companies such as Microsoft and Netscape. Web developers look to the W3C to establish standards and introduce new Web technologies. The W3C is responsible for maintaining and guiding HTML standards.

HTML Versions

The most recent version of HTML is version 4. Version 4 allows for separate formatting instructions, called cascading style sheets (CSS), and other presentation controls. By moving all the formatting controls to style sheets, HTML 4 frees up the Web developer to assign formatting to not only paragraphs of text, but also to the entire page or every page on the Web site. Moving formatting to a separate style sheet makes it easier to maintain other coding on the HTML document.

HTML Evolution

Seeing a need for additional structure for HTML documents, the W3C next introduced XML (*Extensible Markup Language*). XML is a meta-markup language for creating other languages; however, it is not as lenient as HTML, so the W3C rewrote HTML in XML and called it XHTML. XHTML has all the features of HTML, but gains XML's power and flexibility.

XHTML

Although XHTML is technically an XML application, it closely copies much of HTML 4 — so much so, that many view XHTML as a stricter version of HTML. With XHTML, you cannot leave off tags, and the order of tags is strictly enforced. Tags are closed in the reverse order in which they were opened. You must also write XHTML coding in lowercase letters, and all attributes must be enclosed in quotes. These are just a few examples of code-writing details users must follow to create XHTML documents.

HTML Versus XHTML

Version 4 is the last version of HTML the W3C will introduce. The future of Web page development lies in XHTML. However, billions of Web pages are already written in HTML, and browser support is more common for HTML, so HTML documents are not likely to go away for quite some time. If you learn HTML, the transition to XHTML is an easy one, requiring only a dedication to detail when writing well-formed code.

Explore Web Browsers

Web browsers are designed to read HTML instructions and display the content on your screen. You can use a browser to display HTML files you save on your computer, called *local pages*, or HTML pages transferred through a Web server. You can also use a browser to test your HTML pages.

Browser Discrepancies

There are many different Web browsers around today, and numerous versions of each. Each browser interprets HTML code in its own way, which means Web pages do not always appear the same from one browser to another. HTML standardization helps alleviate some of the discrepancies, but not all. For this reason, you need to write clean, well-formed HTML code and be sure to test your pages in different browsers to see the varying results.

Finding Browsers

Microsoft Internet Explorer (www.microsoft.com/ie) and Netscape Navigator (www.netscape.com) are the two most popular browsers available today. You should also test your pages in a few of the lesser-known browsers, such as Opera (www.opera.com) and Amaya (www.w3.org/Amaya/). For a complete list of browsers, visit http://dir.yahoo.com/Computers_and_Internet/Software/Internet/World_Wide_Web/Browsers.

Explore HTML Editors

In the early days of Web development, plain old text editors were the application of choice. Today, you can use a variety of programs to write your HTML code.

Simple Text Editors

Simple text editors, also called plain-text editors, are easy to find. Most computers come with one, such as Windows Notepad. You can also find shareware and freeware versions on the Internet, such as TextPad, EditPad Lite, and UltraEdit. Simple text editors offer no-frills word processing and are often the best choice for writing HTML code.

Word Processing Programs

You can also use word processing programs, such as Microsoft Word, to write HTML. Use caution, however, because commercial word processors can store extraneous information with your files, some of which interferes with HTML.

HTML Editors

HTML editors are dedicated programs for writing HTML code. Microsoft FrontPage and Macromedia Dreamweaver are examples of HTML editors. HTML editors can shield you from learning HTML code in detail by offering a graphical environment for building Web pages. However, most also allow you to switch to text-based editing as well.

Understanding HTML Syntax and Rules

The HTML language is a simple language for describing Web page content. HTML rules, called *syntax*, govern the way in which code is written. Learning the right way to write your code can save you confusion and errors later.

Writing HTML

The instructions you write in HTML are called *tags*. Tags are surrounded by angle brackets, < >. You can write tags in upper- or lowercase letters. Many users prefer to write their tags in uppercase to make them easier to identify on the document page. If you create a page in XHTML, a stricter variation of HTML, you need to use lowercase letters for your tags.

Elements

Elements identify the different parts of your HTML document. For example, <BODY> and </BODY> are tags defining the body text element on a page. The browser reads any text between the two tags as part of the body element. Many elements use tag pairs, an opening and closing tag, such as <P> and </P>, while others, such as the Image tag (<IMG>) do not. Closing tags must always include a slash (/).

Attributes and Values

Each element has unique attributes you can assign. Many attributes require that you set a value, such as a measurement or specification. For example, you can set a paragraph's alignment on the page using the ALIGN attribute, and set a value for the alignment by specifying the value as left, right, or center. For example, the code might read:

```
<P ALIGN="center">
My paragraph text.</P>
```

Values are always enclosed in quotation marks and appear within the element's start tag.

Entities

Any special characters you add to a page, such as a copyright symbol or a fraction, are called *entities*. HTML uses entities to represent characters not readily available on the keyboard. All entities are preceded with an ampersand (&) and ended with a semicolon (;). For example, to add a copyright symbol to your page, the code looks like this:

```
&copy;
```

Avoid Syntax Errors

To avoid HTML errors, always take time to proofread your code. Make sure you have brackets on your tags and that your closing tags include a slash. You must surround any values you define for attributes with quotation marks. It also helps to write your closing tags in reverse order of the opening tags. For example:

```
<P ALIGN="center">
<B>My text.</B></P>
```

To help make your HTML readable, consider using new lines to enter code instead of running everything together on one long line. Using white space can also help, without increasing the file size.

View HTML Code in a Browser

If you generate HTML code using a program, such as Microsoft FrontPage or Macromedia Dreamweaver, the code can appear overwhelmingly complex.

You can view the HTML code for any Web page using your browser window. Viewing other Web developers' code is a good way to learn how to write your own code, and can help you generate new ideas for your own pages. You can also save a Web page to study later.

View HTML Code in a Browser

VIEW THE SOURCE CODE

① Open your browser window to the page you want to view.

② Click **View**.

③ Click **Source** (Internet Explorer) or **Page Source** (Navigator).

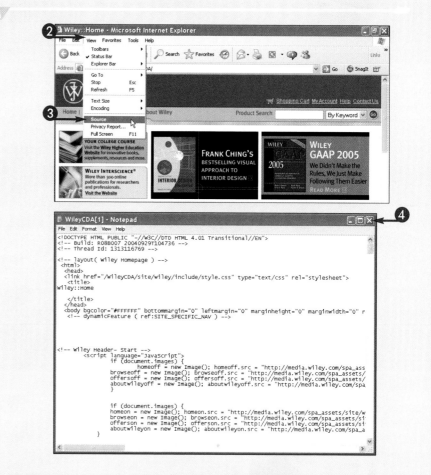

A window appears displaying the HTML source code for the page.

④ Click the **Close** button (⊠) when finished.

The window closes.

SAVE AN HTML DOCUMENT

① With the source code window open, click **File**.

② Click **Save As** (Internet Explorer) or **Save Page As** (Navigator).

The Save As dialog box appears.

③ Navigate to the folder where you want to store the page.

④ Type a name for the page.

⑤ Click **Save**.

The page is saved.

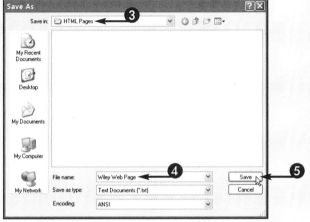

Can I copy the source code from another page?

You can copy HTML code you see on other pages; however, you should always obtain permission to reuse it yourself. Most Web page authors are happy to share their code with others, especially something complex and innovative, but make sure it is okay before attempting to do so.

How do I print the HTML code from the viewer window?

You can print the code from the text viewer window by clicking **File** and clicking **Print**. This opens the Print dialog box, where you can choose a printer or click **Print** to print your code. This technique works in both Internet Explorer and Navigator.

Chapter 2

Creating Your First HTML Page

Are you ready to start creating a Web page?
This chapter shows you how to get started
with a basic HTML document.

Understanding HTML Document Structure

All HTML documents are built on key elements that define a page's structure. Although every HTML page differs in content and layout, the underlying structure remains the same. Understanding the basic structure of a document can help you understand how to build and improve your own HTML pages.

HTML Element

The <HTML> and </HTML> tags are the main tags used to identify an HTML document. When a browser encounters these tags, it knows that anything within the two tags is part of an HTML document. With the latest version of HTML and newer versions of Web browsers, the tags are not always necessary, but adding them is always good form. Older Web browsers expect to see the HTML element tags.

Document Type Declaration

You can add a DOCTYPE declaration to specify the version of HTML upon which the page is based. There are three types of HTML you can declare: HTML 4.0 Transitional, HTML 4.0 Strict, and HTML 4.0 Frameset. The transitional version is the most inclusive, incorporating both structural and presentation elements. The strict version is more pared-down and excludes presentation elements. The frameset version is the same as the transitional version but includes all the elements necessary to make frames on a page.

Document Header

You can use the document header to add basic information about your page. The document header tags, <HEAD> and </HEAD>, follow the <HTML> opening tag. You can use the document header to include title information, metadata, and base and script elements. Learn more about scripts in Chapter 13.

Title

You can add a title to your document header to help others identify your page. For example, if you are building a Web page for a business, your company name is a good page title. Web browsers display the title in the browser window's title bar. You can use the <TITLE> and </TITLE> tags to define a page title. For best results, keep the title brief and to the point.

Metadata

Metadata is data that describes the material on your page, such as author information, any programs you used to create the page, a description of the page, and keywords for search engines. You can use the metadata tags to add author and copyright information, too. You can place metadata between your document header tags.

Body

The content of your page, including paragraphs, lists, and images, appears within the body of your HTML document. The body of the document is identified by the <BODY> and </BODY> tags. Anything you place between these tags appears on the document and in the browser window. The body of the document includes blocks of text, headings, lists, tables, and forms. You learn more about working with body text in Chapter 3.

Start an HTML Document

You can start an HTML document using a text editor or word processing program. You can use sets of HTML tags to define the basic structure of your page.

The **<HTML>**, **<HEAD>**, and **<TITLE>** tags are basic to Web pages. The **<HEAD>** and **<TITLE>** information does not appear on the Web page itself; however, the text you include between these tags declares the type of document and briefly describes the page. The text you place between these tags appears in the browser window's title bar.

Start an HTML Document

① Open the text editor or word processing program you want to use.

Note: See Chapter 1 to learn more about text editors.

② Type **<HTML>**.

This tag declares the document is an HTML document.

③ Press Enter.

Note: See Chapter 1 to learn more about HTML tag sets.

④ Type **<HEAD>**.

This tag starts the information describing the page, including any title text.

⑤ Press Enter.

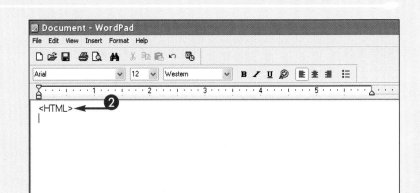

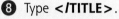
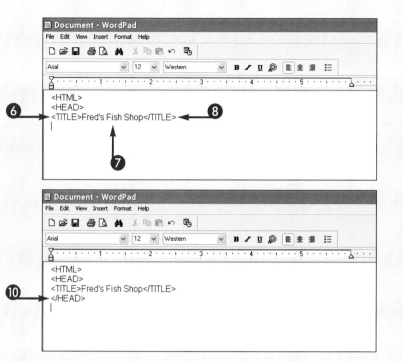

6 Type **<TITLE>**.

7 Type title text for your page.

Title text describes the contents of the page and appears in the Title bar of the Web browser.

8 Type **</TITLE>**.

9 Press Enter.

10 Type **</HEAD>**.

This tag completes the document heading information for the page.

11 Press Enter.

Note: *You do not need to press* Enter *each time you start a new tag or add a close tag. However, placing tags on their own lines in the code can help you more easily identify your page structure.*

Which is faster — typing the content first and then adding tags, or typing everything as I go?
Either method works fine; however, if you are just getting started, you may want to define your tags first and then add the content. This allows you to easily see the insertion of both start and close tags before you add more text to the document. The more text you type, the more difficult it becomes to locate tag errors later.

Does it matter if I type upper- and lowercase letters or all caps for my tags?
No. However, it helps to be consistent with your tags, particularly if you run across an error later. For example, typing tags in all uppercase letters can make it easier to identify the tags on the page.

continued

Start an HTML Document *(continued)*

> You can use the body tags, `<BODY>` and `</BODY>`, to add content to your page. Page content can include lines of text, paragraphs, bulleted and numbered lists, and more.

Start an HTML Document *(continued)*

⑫ Type **<BODY>**.

This tag starts the actual content of your Web page.

⑬ Press Enter.

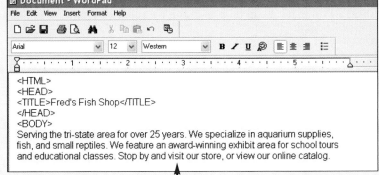

⑭ Type the body text you want to appear on the page.

Body text is the content of your page, including lines of text, paragraphs, lists, and more.

For practice, consider typing a simple paragraph for the body text.

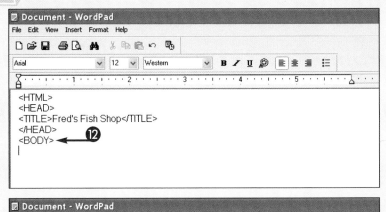

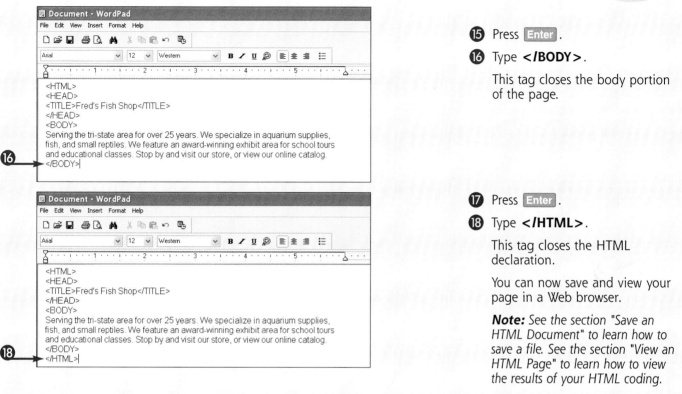

⑮ Press **Enter**.

⑯ Type **</BODY>**.

This tag closes the body portion of the page.

⑰ Press **Enter**.

⑱ Type **</HTML>**.

This tag closes the HTML declaration.

You can now save and view your page in a Web browser.

Note: *See the section "Save an HTML Document" to learn how to save a file. See the section "View an HTML Page" to learn how to view the results of your HTML coding.*

How do I turn off WordPad's text wrapping?

If the text you type in WordPad scrolls off the screen, the text wrapping feature is turned off. You can turn on the text wrapping feature to keep the text in view at all times.

❶ Click **View**.

❷ Click **Options**.

This opens the Options dialog box.

❸ On the **Text** tab, click the **Wrap to window** option (○ changes to ⊙).

❹ Click **OK**.

Text wrapping is now activated.

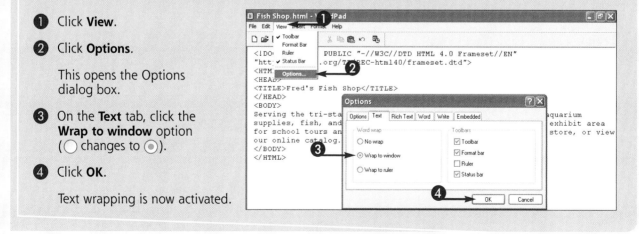

Save an HTML Document

When naming a Web page, do not use spaces and keep your filenames to letters and numbers. If you are creating a main page for a Web site, it is common to name the page index.html or default.htm.

You can save your Web page as an HTML file type so that users can view it in a Web browser. When saving a Web page, you can use the HTML or HTM file extensions.

Save an HTML Document

① Click **File**.

Note: Your text editor may have a different command name for saving files. See your program's documentation for more information.

② Click **Save**.

③ Navigate to the folder or drive where you want to store the file.

● You can click here and select a different folder or drive.

④ Click here and select **Text Document**.

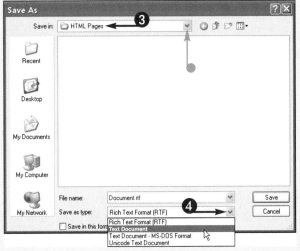

Save As

Save in: HTML Pages

Recent

Desktop

My Documents

My Computer

My Network

File name: FishShop.html ← ⑤

Save as type: Text Document

☐ Save in this format by default

Save ← ⑥

Cancel

⑤ Type a name for the file, followed by **.html** or **.htm**.

⑥ Click **Save**.

WordPad

⚠ You are about to save the document in a Text-Only format, which will remove all formatting. Are you sure you want to do this?

⑦ → Yes   No

A dialog box may appear prompting you that all the formatting will be removed.

⑦ Click **Yes**.

The file is saved.

What is the difference between the .html and .htm suffix?

The shorter suffix, also called a file extension, .htm, is left over from the days of DOS when filenames could utilize only a three-character file extension. Microsoft Windows-based systems still default to the htm extension. If you use a Microsoft program, such as FrontPage, to create an HTML file, it automatically assigns the htm extension. Today's computers can handle much longer filenames and extensions, so the three-character limitation is no longer an issue. Web browsers and servers can read either extension; however, for consistency you might want to stick with .html. The html extension is more universally used with various hosting systems.

What makes a good filename for a Web page?

Any time you name a file, you need to keep the name simple enough so that you can remember it and locate it again later. In addition, because filenames are important when used as hyperlinks and page titles, it is best to utilize a name that makes sense to the type of page you are designing. For example, if you are creating a company Web site, your filenames might use your company name. It is also a good idea to keep your Web page files in one folder and give the folder a name that clearly identifies the content, such as My Web Pages.

View an
HTML Page

After you create and save an HTML document, you can view it in your Web browser. For example, you might view your pages to check how the content or images look in a browser, or you might view pages to look for typing errors.

View an HTML Page

1. Open your Web browser.
2. Click **File**.
3. Click **Open**.

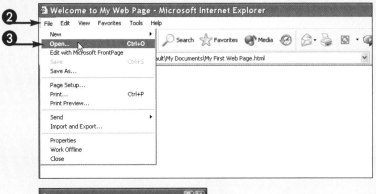

The Open dialog box appears.
4. Click **Browse**.

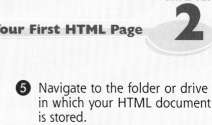

⑤ Navigate to the folder or drive in which your HTML document is stored.

⑥ Click the filename.

⑦ Click **Open**.

● The Open dialog box displays the path and name of the file.

⑧ Click **OK**.

The Web browser displays the page.

● The title information appears here.

● The body information appears here.

Note: *You cannot see metadata information on the browser page.*

Does it matter whether I view a page with Microsoft Internet Explorer or Netscape Navigator?
No. Both browsers are set up to view pages offline as well as online. If you use a browser other than the two mentioned, you may need to follow a different set of steps to open an offline HTML document. Be sure to consult your browser's documentation for more information.

What happens if I cannot view my page?
If you do not see any content for your page, you need to double-check your HTML coding for errors. Make sure your document uses correctly paired start and end tags, and proofread your HTML codes to make sure everything is correct.

Add a Document Declaration

The transitional version of HTML is the most inclusive version you can use. It includes all the standard structural elements as well as presentation elements. The strict version is a streamlined version of the transitional version. The frameset version is the transitional version along with all the necessary frame elements to display frames on a Web page.

You can use a document declaration at the top of your Web page to declare which version of HTML you are using to create the page. You can utilize three types of HTML: HTML 4.0 Transitional, HTML 4.0 Strict, and HTML 4.0 Frameset. The document declaration tags contain a statement declaring the version.

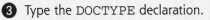

Add a Document Declaration

1 Open the HTML document you want to edit.

2 Insert a new line before the <HTML> tag.

You can press Enter to create a new line.

3 Type the DOCTYPE declaration.

● To specify HTML 4.0 Transitional, type:

<!DOCTYPE HTML PUBLIC "-//W3C// DTD HTML 4.0 Transitional//EN" "http://www.w3.org/TR/REC-html40/ loose.dtd">

You may need to press Enter to continue the coding to a new line.

CHAPTER
2

```
FishShop.html - WordPad
File  Edit  View  Insert  Format  Help

<!DOCTYPE HTML PUBLIC "-//W3C//DTD HTML 4.0 Strict//EN"
"http://www.w3.org/TR/REC-html40/strict.dtd">
<HTML>
<HEAD>
<TITLE>Fred's Fish Shop</TITLE>
</HEAD>
<BODY>
Serving the tri-state area for over 25 years. We specialize in aquarium
supplies, fish, and small reptiles. We feature an award-winning exhibit area
for school tours and educational classes. Stop by and visit our store, or view
our online catalog.
</BODY>
</HTML>
```

```
FishShop.html - WordPad
File  Edit  View  Insert  Format  Help

<!DOCTYPE HTML PUBLIC "-//W3C//DTD HTML 4.0 Frameset//EN"
"http://www.w3.org/TR/REC-html40/frameset.dtd">
<HTML>
<HEAD>
<TITLE>Fred's Fish Shop</TITLE>
</HEAD>
<BODY>
Serving the tri-state area for over 25 years. We specialize in aquarium
supplies, fish, and small reptiles. We feature an award-winning exhibit area
for school tours and educational classes. Stop by and visit our store, or view
our online catalog.
</BODY>
</HTML>
```

● To specify HTML 4.0 Strict, type:

<!DOCTYPE HTML PUBLIC "-//W3C// DTD HTML 4.0 Strict//EN" "http://www.w3.org/TR/REC-html40/ strict.dtd">

● To specify HTML 4.0 Frameset, type:

<!DOCTYPE HTML PUBLIC "-//W3C// DTD HTML 4.0 Frameset//EN" "http://www.w3.org/TR/REC-html40/ frameset.dtd">

The declaration statement is complete.

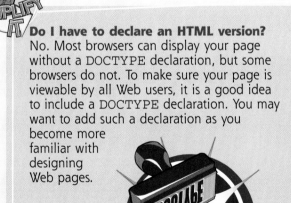

Do I have to declare an HTML version?
No. Most browsers can display your page without a DOCTYPE declaration, but some browsers do not. To make sure your page is viewable by all Web users, it is a good idea to include a DOCTYPE declaration. You may want to add such a declaration as you become more familiar with designing Web pages.

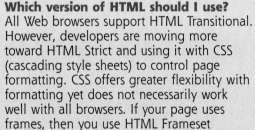

Which version of HTML should I use?
All Web browsers support HTML Transitional. However, developers are moving more toward HTML Strict and using it with CSS (cascading style sheets) to control page formatting. CSS offers greater flexibility with formatting yet does not necessarily work well with all browsers. If your page uses frames, then you use HTML Frameset because it allows you to add frames to a page. Deciding which version to use really depends on what Web page elements you plan to use.

Add Metadata

Keywords and page descriptions are the most common data Web developers enter into the metadata tags. However, metadata is also a great source for other Web page developers, enabling them to see who you are and what sort of notes or techniques you applied to create your page.

You can use metadata to give more details about your page, such as a page description, authoring information, copyrights, keywords, and more. Although metadata does not appear on the Web page itself, the information you insert in the metadata tags is useful with search engines that glean information about your page.

Add Metadata

ADD AN AUTHOR NAME

① Click between the <HEAD> and </HEAD> tags to start a new line.

In this example, the metadata appears below the <TITLE> tags.

② Type **<META NAME = "author"** and a blank space.

③ Type **CONTENT = "My Name">**, replacing *My Name* with your name.

④ Press Enter.

ADD A PAGE DESCRIPTION

⑤ Type **<META NAME = "description"** and a blank space.

⑥ Type **CONTENT = "Page Description">**, replacing *Page Description* with your own page description.

⑦ Press Enter.

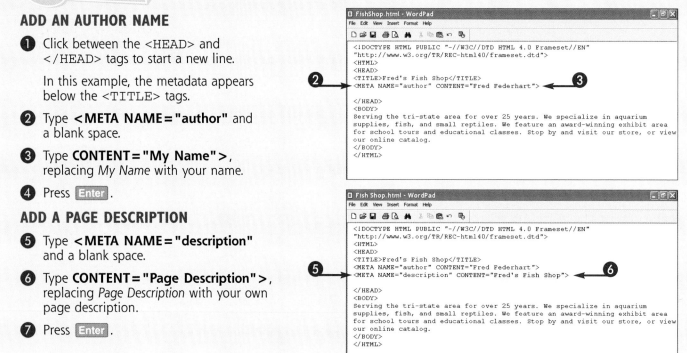

```
Fish Shop.html - WordPad
File  Edit  View  Insert  Format  Help
<!DOCTYPE HTML PUBLIC "-//W3C//DTD HTML 4.0 Frameset//EN"
"http://www.w3.org/TR/REC-html40/frameset.dtd">
<HTML>
<HEAD>
<TITLE>Fred's Fish Shop</TITLE>
<META NAME="author" CONTENT="Fred Federhart">
<META NAME="description" CONTENT="Fred's Fish Shop">
<META NAME="keywords" CONTENT="fish, aquariums, fish supplies, fish exhibit,
small reptiles, freshwater fish, saltwater fish, fish tank supplies">

</HEAD>
<BODY>
Serving the tri-state area for over 25 years. We specialize in aquarium
supplies, fish, and small reptiles. We feature an award-winning exhibit area
for school tours and educational classes. Stop by and visit our store, or view
our online catalog.
</BODY>
</HTML>
```

8 ➤

➤ 9

```
Fish Shop.html - WordPad
File  Edit  View  Insert  Format  Help
<!DOCTYPE HTML PUBLIC "-//W3C//DTD HTML 4.0 Frameset//EN"
"http://www.w3.org/TR/REC-html40/frameset.dtd">
<HTML>
<HEAD>
<TITLE>Fred's Fish Shop</TITLE>
<META NAME="author" CONTENT="Fred Federhart">
<META NAME="description" CONTENT="Fred's Fish Shop">
<META NAME="keywords" CONTENT="fish, aquariums, fish supplies, fish exhibit,
small reptiles, freshwater fish, saltwater fish, fish tank supplies">
<META NAME="copyright" CONTENT="2004">

</HEAD>
<BODY>
Serving the tri-state area for over 25 years. We specialize in aquarium
supplies, fish, and small reptiles. We feature an award-winning exhibit area
for school tours and educational classes. Stop by and visit our store, or view
our online catalog.
</BODY>
</HTML>
```

11 ➤   12 ➤

SPECIFY KEYWORDS

8 Type **<META NAME="keywords"** and a blank space.

9 Type **CONTENT="My Keywords">**, replacing *My Keywords* with a keyword.

For multiple keywords, use a space and commas to separate each keyword.

10 Press **Enter**.

ADD A COPYRIGHT

11 Type **<META NAME="copyright"** and a blank space.

12 Type **CONTENT="2004">**, replacing *2004* with your own numbers or copyright information.

13 Press **Enter**.

The copyright statement is now a part of the document.

How do I add the name of the program I used to design my page to the metadata information?
To specify an authoring program, type **<META NAME="generator" CONTENT="Program Name">**. Substitute your own program name for the text *"Program Name"*.

Who can view my metadata?
The only time anyone can see your metadata information is if they view the HTML code for the page. To view the HTML coding of any page in your browser window, click **View** and then click **Source**. This opens your text editor window and you can see the HTML used to create the page. Any metadata assigned to the document appears at the top, within the <HEAD> and </HEAD> tags.

Chapter 3

Adding Text

Are you ready to begin entering text to build your Web page content? This chapter shows you how to add different types of text elements to a document.

Create a New Paragraph

You can use paragraph tags to start new paragraphs in an HTML document. In a word processing program, you press the Enter or Return key to start a new line. Web browsers do not read these line breaks. Instead, you must insert a <P> tag any time you want to start a new paragraph in your Web page.

Paragraphs are left aligned by default, but you can use the align tags to change the horizontal alignment of text. See the section "Change Paragraph Alignment" to learn more.

Create a New Paragraph

① Type **<P>** in front of the text you want to create as a new paragraph.

② Type **</P>** at the end of the paragraph.

When displayed in a Web browser, the text appears as a paragraph with extra space before and after the block of text.

Change Paragraph Alignment

You can use the **ALIGN** attribute within numerous tag elements, including headings, lists, and more.
For example, you can center a heading or right-align a bulleted list.

You can control the horizontal positioning, or alignment, of your paragraphs using the align tags. You can choose to align a paragraph to the left, right, center, or justify the text to create both a left and right alignment with the margins. Paragraphs are left aligned by default unless you specify another alignment.

Change Paragraph Alignment

① Click inside the **<P>** tag in which you want to change alignment.

② Type **ALIGN = "?"**, replacing the *?* with **Left**, **Center**, **Right**, or **Justify**.

Note: *You can type HTML commands in upper- and lower-case letters, or a mixture of both.*

When displayed in a Web browser, the text aligns as specified.

● In this example, the line of text is centered on the page.

Add a Line Break

You can use the break tag, <BR>, to create a line break to start a new line of text. Ordinarily, Web browsers wrap text automatically so it continues to the next line when the current line reaches the right side of the browser window. You can insert a line break to instruct the browser to break the text to a new line. Line breaks give you control over where the text breaks.

You can also use the <BR> tag to add extra blank lines between paragraphs. This is useful if you want to add extra space above or below a block of text or heading.

Add a Line Break

① Type **
** in front or at the end of each line of text that you want to appear as a new line.

You can also type the tag at the end of a line of text.

Note: *You do not need a close tag for the <BR> tag.*

● When displayed in a Web browser, each instance of the tag creates a new text line.

Shakespeare Quotes.html – WordPad
File Edit View Insert Format Help

```
<HTML>
<HEAD>
<TITLE>My Favorite Quotes</TITLE>
</HEAD>
<BODY>

My Favorite Shakespeare Poems and Quotes

<P>Sonnet 18
<BR>Shall I compare thee to a summer's day?
<BR>Thou art more lovely and more temperate:
<BR>Rough winds do shake the darling buds of May,
<BR>And summer's lease hath all too short a date.
</P>
</BODY>
</HTML>
```

My Favorite Quotes – Microsoft Internet Explorer
File Edit View Favorites Tools Help

Back · · Search Favorites Media · · · Links

Address C:\Documents and Settings\default\My Documents\HTML Pages\Shakespeare Quotes.html Go SnagIt

My Favorite Shakespeare Poems and Quotes

Sonnet 18

Shall I compare thee to a summer's day?
Thou art more lovely and more temperate:
Rough winds do shake the darling buds of May,
And summer's lease hath all too short a date.

Insert a
Blank Space

You can insert blank spaces within a line of text to create indents or add emphasis to the text. You can also use blank spaces to help position elements on a Web page, such as a graphic or photo.

Insert a Blank Space

① Type ** ** in the line where you want to add a blank space.

To add multiple spaces, type the code multiple times.

The browser displays blank spaces in the line.

● In this example, the blank spaces create an indent for a paragraph.

Insert
Preformatted Text

You can use the preformatted tags, **<PRE>** and **</PRE>**, to keep the line breaks and spaces you enter for a paragraph or block of text. Web browsers ignore hard returns, line breaks, or extra spaces between words unless you insert the preformatted text element tags. If you type a paragraph with spacing just the way you want it, you can assign the preformatted tags to keep the spacing in place.

Insert Preformatted Text

1 Type **<PRE>** above the text you want to keep intact.

2 Type **</PRE>** below the text.

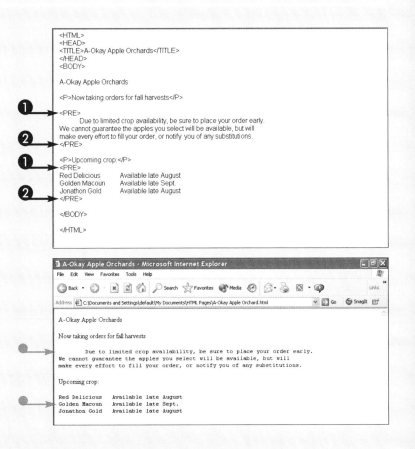

* When displayed in a Web browser, the text retains all the white space you originally added to the text.

Insert a Heading

You can use the **ALIGN** element to change the horizontal alignment of a heading, such as **<H1 ALIGN= "right">**. See the section "Change Paragraph Alignment" to learn more about inserting alignment controls with your text.

You can use headings to help clarify information on a page, organize text, and create visual structure. You can choose from six different heading levels for a document, ranging from heading level 1 (**<H1>**), the largest, to heading level 6 (**<H6>**), the smallest. Headings appear as bold type on a Web page.

Insert a Heading

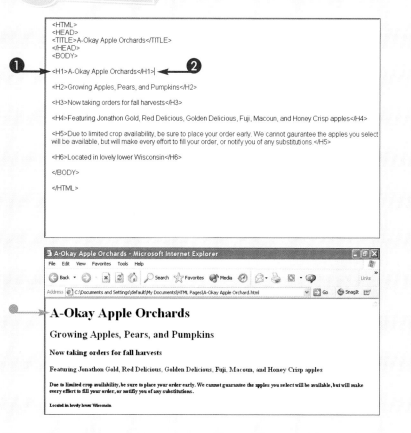

```
<HTML>
<HEAD>
<TITLE>A-Okay Apple Orchards</TITLE>
</HEAD>
<BODY>

<H1>A-Okay Apple Orchards</H1>

<H2>Growing Apples, Pears, and Pumpkins</H2>

<H3>Now taking orders for fall harvests</H3>

<H4>Featuring Jonathon Gold, Red Delicious, Golden Delicious, Fuji, Macoun, and Honey Crisp apples</H4>

<H5>Due to limited crop availability, be sure to place your order early. We cannot gaurantee the apples you select
will be available, but will make every effort to fill your order, or notify you of any substitutions </H5>

<H6>Located in lovely lower Wisconsin</H6>

</BODY>

</HTML>
```

① Type **<H?>** in front of the text you want to turn into a heading, replacing the *?* with the heading level number you want to assign.

You can set a heading level from 1 to 6.

② Type **</H?>** at the end of the heading text, replacing the *?* with the corresponding heading level you assign.

● The heading appears in bold text in the Web browser.

This figure shows an example of each heading size in descending order.

Add Block Quotes

You can use block quotes to set off a paragraph from the rest of the document page. Block quotes are commonly used with quoted text or excerpts from other sources.

Add Block Quotes

1 Type **<BLOCKQUOTE>** in front of the text you want to turn into a block quote.

2 Type **</BLOCKQUOTE>** at the end of the text.

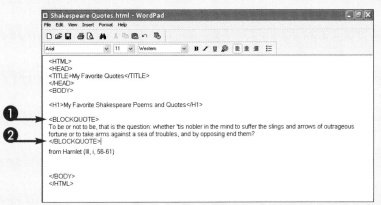

● The Web browser displays the block quote as inset text on the document page.

Insert a Comment

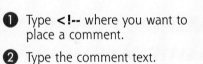

You can use comments to write notes to yourself within an HTML document. Comments do not appear on the actual Web page. For example, you might leave a comment about a future editing task, or leave a note to other Web developers viewing your HTML source code.

Insert a Comment

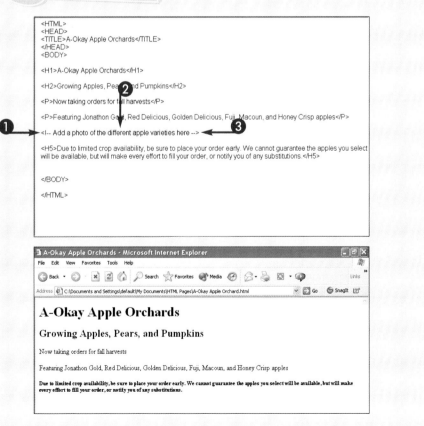

1 Type **<!--** where you want to place a comment.

2 Type the comment text.

3 Type **-->**.

The comment does not appear on the page when viewed in a Web browser.

Create a Numbered List

> You can use numbered lists in your Web page to display all kinds of ordered lists. For example, you can use numbered lists to show steps or prioritize items.

Create a Numbered List

PLACE TEXT IN A NUMBERED LIST

1 Type **<OL>** above the text you want to turn into a numbered list.

2 Type **<LI>** in front of each item in the list.

3 Type **</LI>** after each list item.

4 Type **</OL>** after the list text.

```
<HTML>
<HEAD>
<TITLE>A-Okay Apple Orchards</TITLE>
</HEAD>
<BODY>

<H1>A-Okay Apple Orchards</H1>

<H2>Growing Apples, Pears, and Pumpkins</H2>

<P>Now taking orders for fall harvests</P>

<P>Featuring Jonathon Gold, Red Delicious, Golden Delicious, Fuji, Macoun, and Honey Crisp apples</P>

<!-- Add a photo of the different apple varieties here -->

<P>How to Order:</P>
<OL>
<LI>Specify an apple variety, pear variety, or pumpkin type and size </LI>
<LI>Fill out your shipping information.</LI>
<LI>Select a payment method.</LI>
<LI>Submit your order.</LI>
<LI>Receive a confirmation e-mail.</LI>
</OL>

<H5>Due to limited crop availability, be sure to place your order early. We cannot guarantee the apples you select will be available, but will make every effort to fill your order, or notify you of any substitutions.</H5>
```

● The text appears as a numbered list on the Web page.

A-Okay Apple Orchards

Growing Apples, Pears, and Pumpkins

Now taking orders for fall harvests

Featuring Jonathon Gold, Red Delicious, Golden Delicious, Fuji, Macoun, and Honey Crisp apples

How to Order:

1. Specify an apple variety, pear variety, or pumpkin type and size.
2. Fill out your shipping information.
3. Select a payment method.
4. Submit your order.
5. Receive a confirmation e-mail.

Due to limited crop availability, be sure to place your order early. We cannot guarantee the apples you select will be available, but will make every effort to fill your order, or notify you of any substitutions.

```
<HTML>
<HEAD>
<TITLE>A-Okay Apple Orchards</TITLE>
</HEAD>
<BODY>

<H1>Kinkoph Designs</H1>

<H2>Table of Contents</H2>
<OL TYPE="A">
<LI>Welcome</LI>
<LI>Company History</LI>
<LI>Mission Statement</LI>
<LI>Goals</LI>
<LI>Manufacturing Process</LI>
<LI>Product Descriptions</LI>
<LI>Contact and Ordering Information</LI>
</OL>

</BODY>

</HTML>
```

Kinkoph Designs

Table of Contents

A. Welcome
B. Company History
C. Mission Statement
D. Goals
E. Manufacturing Process
F. Product Descriptions
G. Contact and Ordering Information

SET A NUMBER STYLE

1 Type **TYPE="?"** within the <OL> tag, replacing the ? with a number style code:

A: A, B, C

a: a, b, c

I: I, II, III

I: i, ii, iii

1: 1, 3, 3

The numbered list displays the style you selected.

● In this example, the list is numbered by letters rather than numbers.

How do I add another item to my numbered list?
Simply insert the text where you want it to appear in the list and add the <LI> and </LI> tags before and after the text. The Web browser displays the new list order the next time you view the page.

How do I start my numbered list with a different numbering than the default numbering?
By default, a Web browser reads your numbered list coding and starts with the number 1. To start with a different number, you must add a START attribute to the <OL> tag. For example, to start the numbering at 5, the coding would read <OL START="5" TYPE="1">.

Create a Bulleted List

By default, bulleted lists appear with solid bullets on a Web page. If you want to utilize another bullet style, you must add an attribute to the <UL> tag.

You can add a bulleted list to your document to set apart a list of items from the rest of the page of text. Also called an unordered list, you can use a bulleted list when you do not need to show the items in a particular order.

Create a Bulleted List

PLACE TEXT IN A BULLETED LIST

1. Type **<UL>** above the text you want to turn into a numbered list.

2. Type **<LI>** in front of each item in the list.

3. Type **</LI>** after each list item.

4. Type **</UL>** after the list text.

The text appears as a bulleted list on the Web page.

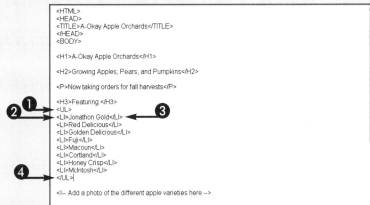

```
<HTML>
<HEAD>
<TITLE>A-Okay Apple Orchards</TITLE>
</HEAD>
<BODY>

<H1>A-Okay Apple Orchards</H1>

<H2>Growing Apples, Pears, and Pumpkins</H2>

<P>Now taking orders for fall harvests</P>

<H3>Featuring:</H3>
<UL>
<LI>Jonathon Gold</LI>
<LI>Red Delicious</LI>
<LI>Golden Delicious</LI>
<LI>Fuji</LI>
<LI>Macoun</LI>
<LI>Cortland</LI>
<LI>Honey Crisp</LI>
<LI>McIntosh</LI>
</UL>

<!-- Add a photo of the different apple varieties here -->

<P>How to Order.</P>
<OL >
```

A-Okay Apple Orchards

Growing Apples, Pears, and Pumpkins

Now taking orders for fall harvests

Featuring:

- Jonathon Gold
- Red Delicious
- Golden Delicious
- Fuji
- Macoun
- Cortland
- Honey Crisp
- McIntosh

How to Order:

1. Specify an apple variety, pear variety, or pumpkin type and size.
2. Fill out your shipping information.
3. Select a payment method.

```
<HTML>
<HEAD>
<TITLE>A-Okay Apple Orchards</TITLE>
</HEAD>
<BODY>

<H1>A-Okay Apple Orchards</H1>

<H2>Growing Apples, Pears, and Pumpkins</H2>

<P>Now taking orders for fall harvests</P>

<H3>Featuring:</H3>
<UL TYPE="square">
<LI>Jonathon Gold</LI>
<LI>Red Delicious</LI>
<LI>Golden Delicious</LI>
<LI>Fuji</LI>
<LI>Macoun</LI>
<LI>Cortland</LI>
<LI>Honey Crisp</LI>
<LI>McIntosh</LI>
</UL>

<!-- Add a photo of the different apple varieties here -->

<P>How to Order:</P>
<OL>
```

A-Okay Apple Orchards

Growing Apples, Pears, and Pumpkins

Now taking orders for fall harvests

Featuring:

- Jonathon Gold
- Red Delicious
- Golden Delicious
- Fuji
- Macoun
- Cortland
- Honey Crisp
- McIntosh

How to Order:

1. Specify an apple variety, pear variety, or pumpkin type and size.
2. Fill out your shipping information.
3. Select a payment method.

SET A BULLET STYLE

1 Type **TYPE="?"** within the `<UL>` tag, replacing the *?* with a bullet style code:

circle: ○

disc: ●

square: ■

The bulleted list displays the style you selected.

● In this example, the bulleted list uses square bullets.

Can I stop a bulleted list for one line of text, and continue the bullets again for the next line?

Yes. If you leave off the `<LI>` and `</LI>` tags for a line of text within the list, a Web browser reads the line as regular text. However, you can insert a line break (`<BR>`) or use the paragraph or heading tags before the non-bulleted text line so that it appears as a separate line in the list. For example:

```
<UL>
<LI>Dogs</LI>
<LI>Cats</LI>
<BR>Birds
<LI>Reptiles</LI>
</UL>
```

Insert Special Characters

Special characters use number or name codes preceded by an ampersand and ending with a semicolon, such as ⅓ for the fraction ½ or ¶ for a paragraph symbol.

You can use HTML code to insert special characters into your Web page text. Special characters are characters that do not appear on your keyboard.

Insert Special Characters

① Click where you want to insert a special character.

② Type the number or name code for the character, with an ampersand (&) before the code and a semicolon (;) following the code.

● The Web browser displays the designated character in the text.

```
<TITLE>A-Okay Apple Orchards</TITLE>
</HEAD>
<BODY>

<H1 ALIGN="center">A-Okay&reg; Apple Orchards</H1>

<H3 ALIGN="center">Growing Apples, Pears, and Pumpkins</H3>
<BR>
<BR>
<BR>

<H2>Want to know more about our various apple varieties?</H2>

<DL>
<DT>Honey Crisp</DT>
<DD>Developed from a 1960 cross of Macoun and Honeygold apples, the goal in creating this apple was to
develop a variety that could withstand difficult winters without losing fruit quality. Skin is mostly red with a yellow
background, while the surface has shallow dimples and dots; sweet, crunchy, and crisp, the flavor ranges from
mild to strongly aromatic, depending on degree of maturity; flesh is cream-colored and coarse.</DD>
<DT>Cortland</DT>
<DD>Sweet, juicy, and just a hint of tartness, this apple is known for its tender snow white flesh. Good for eating
and baking.</DD>
</DL>

</BODY>

</HTML>
```

A-Okay® Apple Orchards

Growing Apples, Pears, and Pumpkins

Want to know more about our various apple varieties?

Honey Crisp
    Developed from a 1960 cross of Macoun and Honeygold apples, the goal in creating this apple was to develop a variety that could withstand difficult winters without losing fruit quality. Skin is mostly red with a yellow background, while the surface has shallow dimples and dots; sweet, crunchy, and crisp, the flavor ranges from mild to strongly aromatic, depending on degree of maturity; flesh is cream-colored and coarse.
Cortland
    Sweet, juicy, and just a hint of tartness, this apple is known for its tender snow white flesh. Good for eating and baking.

Special Characters

To properly insert a character into your Web page text, you need to know the code. The following table gives a list of the common special characters you can insert. For more on inserting these special characters, see the section "Insert Special Characters."

Special Characters					
Description	*Special Character*	*Code*	*Description*	*Special Character*	*Code*
copyright	©	&#169;	small o, slash	ø	&#248;
registered trademark	®	&#174;	em dash	—	&#8212;
trademark	™	&#8482;	en dash	–	&#8211;
paragraph mark	¶	&#182;	micro sign	>	&#181;
quotation mark	"	&#34;	macron	µ	&#175;
left angle quote	«	&#171;	superscript one	¹	&#185;
right angle quote	»	&#187;	superscript two	²	&#178;
ampersand	&	&#38;	superscript three	³	&#179;
inverted exclamation	¡	&#161;	one-half fraction	½	&#189;
inverted question mark	¿	&#191;	one-fourth fraction	¼	&#188;
broken vertical bar	¦	&#166;	three-fourths fraction	¾	&#190;
section sign	§	&#167;	degree sign	°	&#186;
not sign	¬	&#172;	multiply sign	×	&#215;
umlaut	¨	&#168;	division sign	÷	&#247;
acute accent	´	&#180;	plus or minus sign	±	&#177;
cedilla	¸	&#184;	less-than sign	<	&#60;
bullet	•	&#8226;	greater-than sign	>	&#62;
capital N, tilde	Ñ	&#209;	dagger	†	&#8224;
small n, tilde	ñ	&#241;	double-dagger	‡	&#8225;
capital A, tilde	Ã	&#195;	cent sign	¢	&#162;
small a, tilde	ã	&#227;	pound sterling	£	&#163;
capital A, grave accent	À	&#192;	euro	€	&#8363;
small a, grave accent	à	&#224;	yen sign	¥	&#165;
capital O, slash	Ø	&#216;	general currency	¤	&#164;

Chapter 4

Formatting Text

You can apply numerous formatting tags to control the appearance of text on your Web page. This chapter shows you how to utilize attributes and tags to make your text look its best.

Make Text Bold

You can add bold formatting to your text to give it more emphasis or make your page more visually appealing. For example, you might make a company name bold in a paragraph or add bold to a list of items.

Make Text Bold

① Type **<B>** in front of the text you want to make bold.

② Type **</B>** at the end of the text.

● When displayed in a Web browser, the text appears as bold.

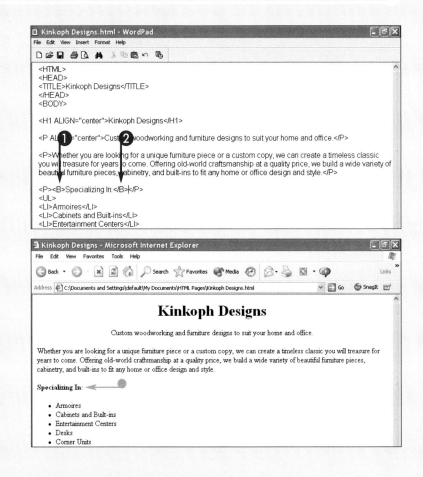

Italicize Text

Common uses for italicized text include emphasizing a new term or setting apart the title of a literary work.

You can add italics to your text to give it more emphasis or make your page more visually appealing. For example, you might make a description under a heading italic to distinguish it from the rest of the page.

Italicize Text

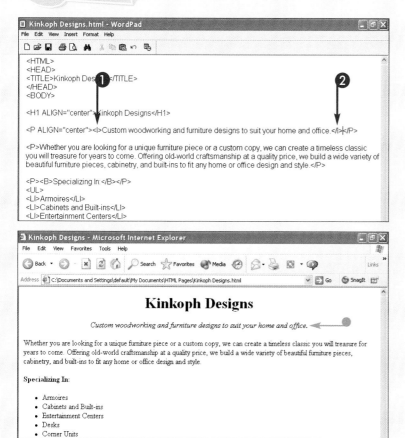

1 Type **<I>** in front of the text you want to italicize.

2 Type **</I>** at the end of the text.

● When displayed in a Web browser, the text appears in italics.

Add Underlining to Text

You can add underlining to your text for added emphasis. For example, you might underline a term or an important name.

Use caution when applying underlining to Web pages, however, as some users will mistake the underlined text for a hyperlink. See Chapter 6 to learn more about using links in Web pages.

Add Underlining to Text

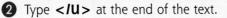

① Type **< U >** in front of the text you want to underline.

② Type **< /U >** at the end of the text.

```
Kinkoph_Designs3.html - WordPad
File  Edit  View  Insert  Format  Help

<TITLE>Kinkoph Designs</TITLE>
</HEAD>
<BODY>

<H1 ALIGN="center">Kinkoph Designs</H1>

<P ALIGN="center"><B><I>Custom woodworking and furniture designs to suit your home and office.</I></B>
</P>

<P><B>Whether you are looking for a unique furniture piece or a custom copy, we can create a timeless classic you will treasure for years to come. Offering old-world craftsmanship at a quality price, we build a wide variety of beautiful furniture pieces, cabinetry, and built-ins to fit any home or office design and style.</B></P>

<P><B><U>Specializing In:</U></B></P>
<UL>
<LI>Armoires</LI>
<LI>Cabinets and Built-ins</LI>
<LI>Entertainment Centers</LI>
<LI>Desks</LI>
```

● The text appears underlined on the Web page.

Change Fonts

You can change the font of your text using the Font tags, **<FONT>** and **</FONT>**, along with the **FACE** attribute. You can use the attribute to specify a font by name.

Not all Web browsers can display a variety of fonts. It is best to assign common fonts typically found on computers, such as Times New Roman and Arial. It is also a good idea to list more than one font name in the FACE attribute, in case the first font is not available on the viewer's computer.

Change Fonts

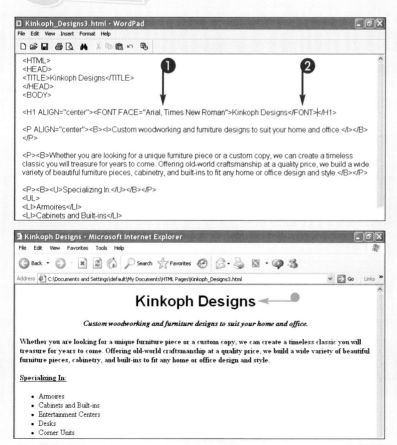

1 Type **<FONT FACE="Arial, Times New Roman">** in front of the text you want to change.

You can substitute different font names for those listed in quotes.

In case the first font you list is not available on the user's computer, list a second font as an alternative.

2 Type **</FONT>** at the end of the text.

● The text appears with a font change on the Web page.

Change Font Size

You can use the **SIZE** attribute to set a new size for a section of text or you can use the **<BASEFONT>** tag to change the font size for the entire page. Keep in mind that the font size you specify may not always display properly in all Web browsers.

You can change the font size for your Web page text using the **SIZE** attribute. HTML coding categorizes fonts into seven different sizes for Web pages. Font Size 1, the smallest, sets your text to 8-point, while Font Size 7, the largest, sets your text to 36-point. The exact point size may vary between browsers, but the size variations are consistent — Font Size 1 is always the smallest text, while Font Size 7 is always the largest.

Change Font Size

CHANGE A SECTION OF TEXT

① Type **<FONT SIZE="?">** in front of the text you want to change, replacing *?* with the size you want to specify, ranging from **1** to **7**.

② Type **</FONT>** at the end of the text.

 The text appears with the designated font size on the Web page.

This figure shows samples of all seven font size levels.

HTML Text Examples.html - WordPad

File   Edit   View   Insert   Format   Help

```
<HTML>
<HEAD>
<TITLE>HTML Text Examples</TITLE>
</HEAD>
<BODY>

<H1>HTML Text Examples</H1>

<P>Font sizes are measured in points, and with HTML coding you can choose from 7 pre-set levels to set a font
size for your text. You can set a font size for a single section of text, or you can set a font size for the entire page.
</P>

<P><FONT SIZE="1">Font Size 1 measures 8 points</FONT></P>
<P><FONT SIZE="2">Font Size 2 measures 10 points</FONT></P>
<P><FONT SIZE="3">Font Size 3 measures 12 points</FONT></P>
<P><FONT SIZE="4">Font Size 4 measures 14 points</FONT></P>
<P><FONT SIZE="5">Font Size 5 measures 18 points</FONT></P>
<P><FONT SIZE="6">Font Size 6 measures 24 points</FONT></P>
<P><FONT SIZE="7">Font Size 7 measures 36 points</FONT></P>

</BODY>

</HTML>
```

HTML Text Examples - Microsoft Internet Explorer

File   Edit   View   Favorites   Tools   Help

Back   •   ×   ②   ⚫   Search   ☆ Favorites   ⚫ Media   ⚫   ☒ • ☒ ☒ • ☒

Address   C:\Documents and Settings\default\My Documents\HTML Pages\HTML Text Examples.html   ☒ ☒ Go   ☺ SnagIt ☒'

HTML Text Examples

Font sizes are measured in points, and with HTML coding you can choose from 7 pre-set levels to set a font size for your text. You can set a font size for a single section of text, or you can set a font size for the entire page.

Font Size 1 measures 8 points

Font Size 2 measures 10 points

Font Size 3 measures 12 points

Font Size 4 measures 14 points

Font Size 5 measures 18 points

Font Size 6 measures 24 points

Font Size 7 measures 36 points

```
HTML Text Examples.html - WordPad
File  Edit  View  Insert  Format  Help

<HTML>
<HEAD>
<TITLE>HTML Text Examples</TITLE>
</HEAD>
<BODY>
<BASEFONT SIZE="4">

<H1>HTML Text Examples</H1>

<P>Font sizes are measured in points, and with HTML coding you can choose from 7 pre-set levels to set a font
size for your text. You can set a font size for a single section of text, or you can set a font size for the entire page.
</P>

<P>Font Size 1 measures 8 points</P>
<P>Font Size 2 measures 10 points</P>
<P>Font Size 3 measures 12 points</P>
<P>Font Size 4 measures 14 points</P>
<P>Font Size 5 measures 18 points</P>
<P>Font Size 6 measures 24 points</P>
<P>Font Size 7 measures 36 points</P>

</BODY>

</HTML>
```

①

```
HTML Text Examples - Microsoft Internet Explorer
File  Edit  View  Favorites  Tools  Help

Back         Search    Favorites   Media              Links
Address  C:\Documents and Settings\default\My Documents\HTML Pages\HTML Text Examples.html      Go    SnagIt
```

HTML Text Examples

Font sizes are measured in points, and with HTML coding you can choose from 7 pre-set levels to set a
font size for your text. You can set a font size for a single section of text, or you can set a font size for
the entire page.

Font Size 1 measures 8 points

Font Size 2 measures 10 points

Font Size 3 measures 12 points

Font Size 4 measures 14 points

Font Size 5 measures 18 points

Font Size 6 measures 24 points

Font Size 7 measures 36 points

CHANGE ALL THE TEXT

① Type **< BASEFONT SIZE = "?" >**
at the top of your Web page text,
replacing *?* with the size you want
to specify, ranging from **1** to **7**.

All the text appears using the new
size in the Web browser.

Note: *The <BASEFONT> tag does
not affect the size of any headings
(<H1>) within your Web page text.*

What font sizes can I apply with the SIZE attribute?

HTML coding sets a range of acceptable font sizes, called
absolute font sizes. These are sizes with proven legibility in
most computers and browsers. Not all browsers apply the
same exact point sizes, but the sizing variations still hold
true—Font Size 1 displays the smallest size to Font Size 7
which displays the largest size.

SIZE Attribute	Font Size	SIZE Attribute	Font Size
Font Size 1	8 points	Font Size 5	18 points
Font Size 2	10 points	Font Size 6	24 points
Font Size 3	12 points	Font Size 7	36 points
Font Size 4	14 points		

Can I set a size other than the recommended size levels?

Yes. You can use relative
font sizes to make variations to the set size
groups. If you type a plus (+) or minus (-)
sign before the size level number, the browser
displays a size relative to the surrounding
text. For example, if you type
<FONT SIZE="+2">,
the browser displays the
text as two sizes larger
than the surrounding
text. If you type
<FONT SIZE=
"-2">, the browser
displays the text two
times smaller than the
surrounding text.

Change the Text Color

Legibility is always a concern when applying color attributes to text. Be sure to choose a color that is easy to read on a Web page. Use caution when applying color text to a color background. Always test your page to make sure the colors do not clash, and your message text remains legible.

You can enhance your text by adding color. The COLOR attribute works along with the <FONT> and </FONT> tags to change the color of text on a page. HTML color is based on hexadecimal values. You can choose from 16 colors.

Change the Text Color

CHANGE A SECTION OF TEXT

❶ Type **<FONT COLOR = "?">** in front of the text you want to change, replacing *?* with the color you want to specify.

You can type the color name or hexadecimal value.

This example shows the hexadecimal value for green. Always precede a hexadecimal value with a # sign.

❷ Type **</FONT>** at the end of the text.

● The text appears with the designated color on the Web page.

CHANGE ALL THE TEXT

1 Within the `<BODY>` tag, type **TEXT="?"**, replacing *?* with the color you want to specify.

You can type the color name or hexadecimal value.

This example uses a color name instead of the hexadecimal value.

All the text appears with the new color in the Web browser.

Note: *The TEXT attribute tag does not affect the link color. To learn more about links, see Chapter 6.*

What colors can I set for my Web page text?
HTML coding uses hexadecimal values for colors, preceded by a number sign (#) followed by a six-digit value, as shown in this table. Browsers can also read some basic colors, including black, white, gray, silver, maroon, red, purple, fuchsia, green, lime, olive, yellow, navy, blue, teal, and aqua. Rather than type a number value, you can type a text value for the color.

Color	Hexadecimal value	Color	Hexadecimal value
Black	#00FFFF	Silver	#C0C0C0
White	#FFFFFF	Navy	#000080
Blue	#0000FF	Fuchsia	#FF00FF
Red	#FF0000	Lime	#00FF00
Yellow	#FFFF00	Maroon	#800000
Green	#008000	Olive	#808000
Purple	#800080	Teal	#008080
Gray	#808080		

Adjust Margins

You can use the margin attributes to control page margins; however, these attributes vary in coding between Internet Explorer and Netscape Navigator. Internet Explorer recognizes the **LEFTMARGIN**, **RIGHTMARGIN**, **TOPMARGIN**, and **BOTTOMMARGIN** attributes. Netscape Navigator recognizes **MARGINWIDTH** and **MARGINHEIGHT**. Be sure to enter both browser types so your page is viewable by all users.

You can adjust the margins of your Web page to change the amount of space that appears at the top, bottom, left, or right edges of the page. By default, the HTML margins are set at approximately 10 pixels. You can adjust the settings to suit the design needs of your page.

Adjust Margins

1 Within the <BODY> tag, type **MARGIN="?"**.

Substitute *MARGIN* with the margin attribute you want to change: **LEFTMARGIN**, **RIGHTMARGIN**, **TOPMARGIN**, **BOTTOMMARGIN**, **MARGINWIDTH**, or **MARGINHEIGHT**.

Substitute the *?* with the amount of indentation you want to create, measured in pixels.

You can set the margin for one side of the page, or all four sides, all within the <BODY> tag.

The Web browser displays your page with the specified margins.

Note: *See Chapter 3 to learn how to change the alignment of text on a page.*

Shakespeare Quotes.html - WordPad

```
<HTML>
<HEAD>
<TITLE>My Favorite Quotes</TITLE>
</HEAD>
<BODY LEFTMARGIN="80" RIGHTMARGIN="80">

<H1>My Favorite Shakespeare Poems and Quotes</H1>

<P>To be or not to be, that is the question: whether 'tis nobler in the mind to suffer the slings and arrows of
outrageous fortune or to take arms against a sea of troubles, and by opposing end them?<BR>
from Hamlet (III, i, 56-61)</P>

<P>All the world's a stage, and all the men and women merely players. They have their exits and their entrances;
And one man in his time plays many parts.<BR>
from As You Like It ( II, Scene VII)</P>

</BODY>
</HTML>
```

My Favorite Quotes - Microsoft Internet Explorer

Address C:\Documents and Settings\default\My Documents\HTML Pages\Shakespeare Quotes.html

My Favorite Shakespeare Poems and Quotes

To be or not to be, that is the question: whether 'tis nobler in the mind to suffer the slings and arrows of outrageous fortune or to take arms against a sea of troubles, and by opposing end them? from Hamlet (III, i, 56-61)

All the world's a stage, and all the men and women merely players. They have their exits and their entrances; And one man in his time plays many parts. from As You Like It (II, Scene VII)

Set a Page Background Color

You can add color to the background of the page using the **BGCOLOR** attribute. Always choose a background color that complements your text.

Set a Page Background Color

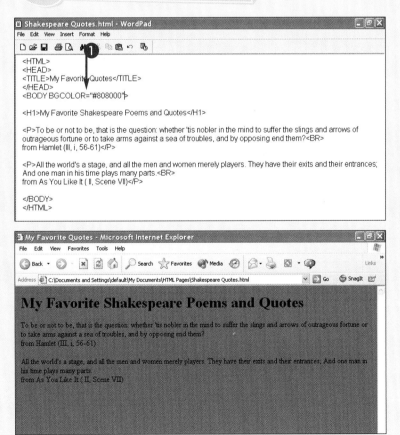

1 Within the <BODY> tag, type **BGCOLOR = "dp?"**.

Substitute *dp* with a color value for the color you want to use, such as **#808000** for olive.

You can also type a color name instead of the hexadecimal value.

Note: See the section "Change the Text Color" for a table of 16 color codes you can apply.

The page appears in the Web browser with a background color assigned.

Add a
Horizontal Line

You can define the thickness and length of a horizontal line using the **SIZE** and **WIDTH** attributes. For example, you can make the line extend across half the page.

You can add a solid horizontal line, or *rule*, across your page to give the page visual interest or break up blocks of information. Horizontal rules must occupy a line by themselves and cannot appear within a paragraph.

Add a Horizontal Line

ADD A SIMPLE LINE

① Type **<HR>** where you want to insert a horizontal rule.

The browser displays the line across the page.

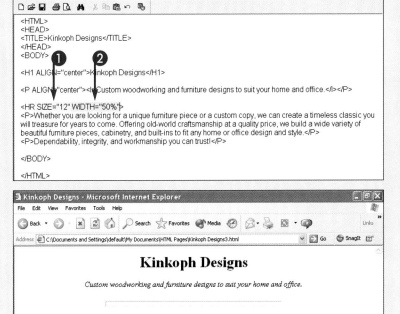

```
Kinkoph Designs3.html - WordPad
File  Edit  View  Insert  Format  Help

<HTML>
<HEAD>
<TITLE>Kinkoph Designs</TITLE>
</HEAD>
<BODY>

<H1 ALIGN="center">Kinkoph Designs</H1>

<P ALIGN="center"><I>Custom woodworking and furniture designs to suit your home and office.</I></P>

<HR SIZE="12" WIDTH="50%">
<P>Whether you are looking for a unique furniture piece or a custom copy, we can create a timeless classic you
will treasure for years to come. Offering old-world craftsmanship at a quality price, we build a wide variety of
beautiful furniture pieces, cabinetry, and built-ins to fit any home or office design and style.</P>
<P>Dependability, integrity, and workmanship you can trust!</P>

</BODY>

</HTML>
```

SET A LINE THICKNESS AND WIDTH

① Within the <HR> tag, type **SIZE="?"**, replacing *?* with the thickness you want to assign, measured in pixels.

② Within the <HR> tag, type **WIDTH="?%"**, replacing *?* with the percentage of the page you want to set the rule across.

The browser displays the line across the page.

```
Kinkoph Designs - Microsoft Internet Explorer
File  Edit  View  Favorites  Tools  Help

Back        Search  Favorites  Media            Links

Address  C:\Documents and Settings\default\My Documents\HTML Pages\Kinkoph Designs3.html       Go      SnagIt
```

Kinkoph Designs

Custom woodworking and furniture designs to suit your home and office.

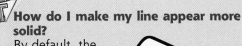

Whether you are looking for a unique furniture piece or a custom copy, we can create a timeless classic you will treasure for years to come. Offering old-world craftsmanship at a quality price, we build a wide variety of beautiful furniture pieces, cabinetry, and built-ins to fit any home or office design and style.

Dependability, integrity, and workmanship you can trust!

How do I make my line appear more solid?

By default, the browser displays horizontal rules with shading, giving the lines a three-dimensional effect. To remove the shading, add the NOSHADE attribute to your <HR> tag, such as <HR NOSHADE>.

Can I add color to a horizontal line?

Yes. You can insert the COLOR attribute and assign a color value to a line. For example, if you type <HR COLOR="#0000FF">, the browser displays the line as blue. See the back of this book for a full color chart you can use to assign colors to Web pages.

Creating Style Sheets

Looking for an easier way to format your Web pages? This chapter shows you how to use style sheets to assign formatting properties and values to your HTML documents.

Understanding Style Sheets

You can use *cascading style sheets,* or CSS, to exercise precise control over the appearance of your HTML documents. Style sheets can help you maintain a consistent look and feel throughout your Web site. By regulating formatting controls to another sheet, you can free up your HTML documents of repetitive coding to concentrate on the main elements that make up your pages.

Defining Style Sheets

A style sheet is simply a separate text file with the .css file extension. Style sheets can also be internal, residing within an HTML document. A style sheet holds formatting codes that control your Web page's appearance. You can use style sheets to change the look of any Web page element, such as paragraphs, lists, backgrounds, and more. Any time you want to apply the formatting to an HTML document, you attach — or *link* — the style sheet to the page.

Style Sheets Can Control Multiple Pages

You can link every page in your Web site to a single style sheet. Any changes you make to the style sheet formatting are reflected in every HTML document linking to the sheet. By storing all the formatting information in one convenient spot, you can easily update the appearance of your site's pages in one fell swoop. This can be a real time-saver if your site consists of lots of pages.

Style Sheet Syntax

Style sheets are made up of rules, and each rule has two distinct parts: selectors and declarations. A *selector* specifies the element to which you want to apply a style rule. The *declaration* specifies the formatting for the selector. For example, in the style rule H2 {color: silver}, H2 is the selector and the declaration sets the color property to silver. Declarations can include a property and a value. If you attach a page to the rule H2 {color: silver}, all level 2 headings on the page will appear in silver.

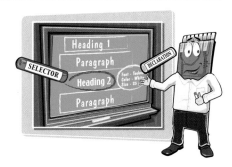

Writing Style Syntax

When writing style sheet syntax, always start with the selector — the element to which you want to apply the rule, followed by the declaration in curly brackets, {}. The declaration consists of a property and a value, and if you use more than one declaration, you must separate each with a semicolon. If you forget to include a semicolon, the browser ignores the rule. To help keep your style sheets readable, consider typing rules and declarations on separate lines. Learn more about writing style rules in Chapter 6.

Style Classes

For times in which you want to apply formatting only to a particular instance of an element, you can use a class attribute. You can assign a distinct name to a class, and add a style rule that applies only to that class. For example, perhaps you want to add select formatting to a paragraph. You define the style rule on your style sheet, and then refer to the class name in your HTML document.

Inheritance

Elements you add within other elements inherit the first element's formatting, unless otherwise specified. For example, if you define a style for the <BODY> element, any elements you nest within the <BODY> element inherit the same formatting. HTML inheritance makes it easy to keep the formatting intact as you add new items within an element.

External and Internal Style Sheets

You can connect an HTML document to an external style sheet or an internal style sheet. *Internal style sheets* exist within an existing HTML page, while *external style sheets* are separate files. External style sheets are used more often because you can link them to more than one HTML document. You might use an internal style sheet if your site consists of a single page.

Create an External
Style Sheet

You can use an external style sheet to define formatting and layout instructions as well as to link the page to your HTML documents. You can save the style sheet as a text file and assign the .css file extension to identify the file as a cascading style sheet.

For more on style sheets and how they work, see the section "Understanding Style Sheets."

Create an External Style Sheet

① Create a new document in your text editor.

Note: *See Chapter 2 to learn how to start and save HTML documents.*

② To create a style rule, type the element tag for which you want to define formatting properties.

This example shows the beginnings of a style rule for defining level 2 headings.

③ Type a space.

④ Type {.

⑤ Type the properties and values for the rule.

Be sure to separate declarations with a semicolon.

In this example, the rule includes setting a font and a font style.

Note: *See Chapter 6 to learn more about writing formatting style rules.*

⑥ Type } to end the rule.

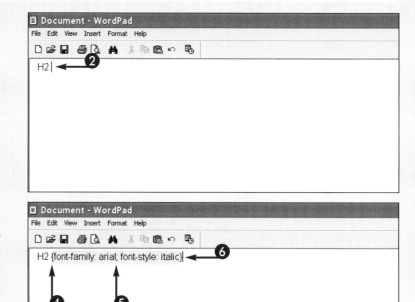

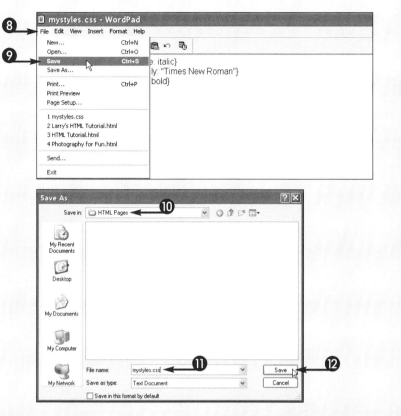

7 Repeat steps **2** through **6** to continue adding style rules to your style sheet.

8 Click **File**.

9 Click **Save**.

The Save As dialog box appears.

10 Navigate to the folder storing your HTML pages.

11 Type a unique filename for your style sheet and the .css extension.

12 Click **Save**.

The new style sheet is saved.

Note: *See the section "Link to a Style Sheet" to learn how to apply a style sheet to your HTML documents.*

Can I use more than one style sheet with my HTML page?

Yes. You can import a style sheet and use the `<STYLE>` tags within the `<HEAD>` tags to reference the sheet. You can import more than one sheet. For example, you can use the code to import two sheets:

```
<STYLE>
@IMPORT URL("?");
@IMPORT URL("?");
</STYLE>
```

Replace the *?* with the location and name of the style sheet. Keep in mind that not all browsers support the `@IMPORT` command.

What is XSL?

XSL, short for *extensible style language*, is a newer style sheet language used with XHTML documents. Because XHTML is a newer markup language version than HTML, XSL is not as widely supported yet as CSS. If you are building your Web pages in XHTML and prefer to use XSL as your style sheet language, be sure to save the text file in the .XSL extension instead of the .CSS extension.

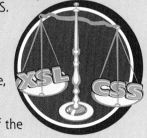

Link to a Style Sheet

See the previous section, "Create an External Style Sheet," to learn how to create and save a style sheet.

You can link to a style sheet to assign the preset formatting to your HTML document. You can link multiple documents to the same style sheet to give all the pages in your site a consistent look and feel.

Link to a Style Sheet

① Open the HTML document you want to link to a style sheet.

Note: See the previous section, "Create an External Style Sheet," to learn how to create a style sheet.

② Click within the <HEAD> and </HEAD> tags and add a new line.

③ Type **<LINK REL="stylesheet" TYPE="text/css"**.

④ Type a blank space and **HREF="?">**, replacing the ? with the name of the style sheet.

The style sheet is now linked with the page.

You can test your page in a browser to see the style sheet results.

Note: See Chapter 2 to learn more.

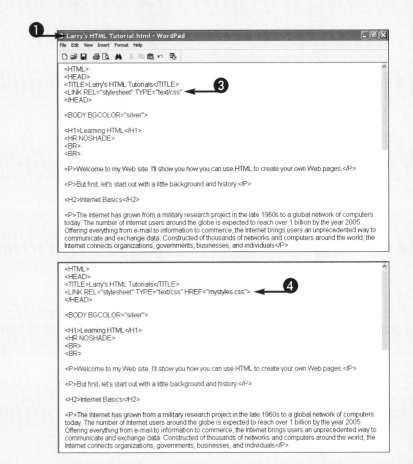

Add Comments to a Style Sheet

You can add comments, or notes, to your style sheet to help you identify your style rules. For example, you might add a comment describing the results of the rule when applied to text. Your Web browser does not read comments.

Add Comments to a Style Sheet

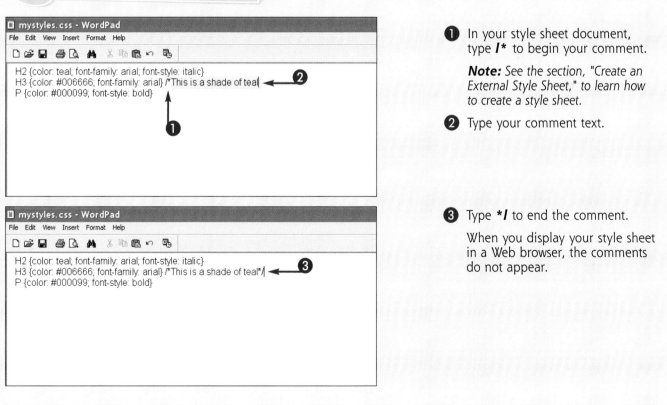

1 In your style sheet document, type **/*** to begin your comment.

Note: See the section, "Create an External Style Sheet," to learn how to create a style sheet.

2 Type your comment text.

3 Type ***/** to end the comment.

When you display your style sheet in a Web browser, the comments do not appear.

Create an Internal Style Sheet

Style Sheet

File Edit View Favorites Tools Help
Back
Address http://www.dessert.com/

Just Desserts

A deliciously different Web site

You can create an internal style sheet that resides within your HTML document. Internal style sheets are handy if your Web site consists of a single page because this allows you to change both style rules and page markup from the same page.

Create an Internal Style Sheet

① Within the <HEAD> and </HEAD> tags, add a new line and type **<STYLE>**.

② Add a new line and type the element tag for which you want to create a style rule.

In this example, a new style rule is created for the H2 element.

③ Type {.

④ Type the properties and values for the rule.

If you intend to add more than one declaration to the rule, be sure to separate declarations with a semicolon.

⑤ Type } to end the rule.

Note: *See Chapter 6 to learn more about writing formatting style rules.*

```
<HTML>
<HEAD>
<TITLE>Larry's HTML Tutorials</TITLE>
<STYLE>
H2
</HEAD>

<BODY BGCOLOR="silver">

<H1>Learning HTML</H1>
<HR NOSHADE>
<BR>
<BR>

<P>Welcome to my Web site. I'll show you how you can use HTML to create your own Web pages.</P>

<P>But first, let's start out with a little background and history.</P>

<H2>Internet Basics</H2>
```

```
<HTML>
<HEAD>
<TITLE>Larry's HTML Tutorials</TITLE>
<STYLE>
H2 {color: teal; font-family: arial; font-style: italic}
</HEAD>

<BODY BGCOLOR="silver">

<H1>Learning HTML</H1>
<HR NOSHADE>
<BR>
<BR>

<P>Welcome to my Web site. I'll show you how you can use HTML to create your own Web pages.</P>

<P>But first, let's start out with a little background and history.</P>

<H2>Internet Basics</H2>
```

```
<HTML>
<HEAD>
<TITLE>Larry's HTML Tutorials</TITLE>
<STYLE>
H2 {color: teal; font-family: arial; font-style: italic}
H3 {color: #006666; font-family: arial}
P {color: #000099; font-style: bold}
</HEAD>


<BODY BGCOLOR="silver">

<H1>Learning HTML</H1>
<HR NOSHADE>
<BR>
<BR>

<P>Welcome to my Web site. I'll show you how you can use HTML to create your own Web pages.</P>

<P>But first, let's start out with a little background and history.</P>

<H2>Internet Basics</H2>

<P>The Internet has grown from a military research project in the late 1960s to a global network of computers
today. The number of Internet users around the globe is expected to reach over 1 billion by the year 2005.
Offering everything from e-mail to information to commerce, the Internet brings users an unprecedented way to
communicate and exchange data. Constructed of thousands of networks and computers around the world, the
Internet connects organizations, governments, businesses, and individuals</P>
```
6

```
<HTML>
<HEAD>
<TITLE>Larry's HTML Tutorials</TITLE>
<STYLE>
H2 {color: teal; font-family: arial; font-style: italic}
H3 {color: #006666; font-family: arial}
P {color: #000099; font-style: bold}
</STYLE>
</HEAD>


<BODY BGCOLOR="silver">

<H1>Learning HTML</H1>
<HR NOSHADE>
<BR>
<BR>

<P>Welcome to my Web site. I'll show you how you can use HTML to create your own Web pages.</P>

<P>But first, let's start out with a little background and history.</P>

<H2>Internet Basics</H2>

<P>The Internet has grown from a military research project in the late 1960s to a global network of computers
today. The number of Internet users around the globe is expected to reach over 1 billion by the year 2005.
Offering everything from e-mail to information to commerce, the Internet brings users an unprecedented way to
communicate and exchange data. Constructed of thousands of networks and computers around the world, the
Internet connects organizations, governments, businesses, and individuals</P>
```
7

6 Repeat steps **2** to **5** to continue adding style rules to your internal style sheet.

7 Add a new line and type **</STYLE>**.

The closing tag completes the style sheet.

You can test your page in a browser to see the style sheet results.

Note: See Chapter 2 to learn more about viewing HTML documents in a browser.

Do older browsers recognize internal style sheets?

Older browsers do not support styles, so they ignore the <STYLE> tags. However, the content of the <STYLE> tag is displayed in older browsers, so any coding you type in between the <STYLE> tags appears on the page. You can prevent an older browser from displaying style tag coding by typing <!-- and --> before and after the style tag details, such as :

<STYLE TYPE = "text/css">

<!--

HR {color: red}
P {margin-left: 20px}

-->

</STYLE>

Can I link another Web page to my internal style sheet?

No. In order for multiple Web pages to take advantage of a style sheet, you must use an external style sheet and link the pages to the sheet. An internal style sheet is useful only for a one-page HTML document. See the section "Create an External Style Sheet" to learn more.

Create a Class

You can set up a class in your external or internal style sheet, and then use the CLASS attribute in your document to assign the properties and values. To learn more about creating external or internal style sheets, see the sections "Create an External Style Sheet" and "Create an Internal Style Sheet."

You can create a class to apply a style rule to certain tags throughout your Web page. For example, if you want all the introductory paragraphs formatted differently than all the regular paragraphs, you can create a class specifically for the introductory paragraphs. Once you create the class, the browser applies it to all the paragraphs to which the class is assigned.

DEFINE A CLASS

① In your external or internal style sheet, type the tag for which you want to create a class.

   Note: See the section "Create an External Style Sheet" to learn more about building style sheets.

② Type a period.

③ Type a name for the class.

④ Type {.

⑤ Type the properties and values for the class.

   If you intend to add more than one declaration to the rule, be sure to separate declarations with a semicolon.

   Note: See Chapter 6 to learn more about writing formatting style rules.

⑥ Type } to end the style rule.

   Your class is now defined.

   If you are editing an external style sheet, save the sheet.

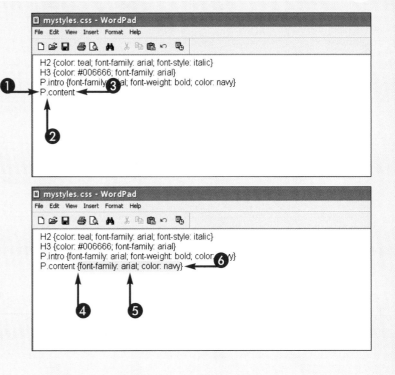

```
<H1>Learning HTML</H1>
<HR NOSHADE>
<BR>
<BR>

<P>Welcome to my Web site. I'll show you how you can use HTML to create your own Web pages.</P>

<P>But first, let's start out with a little background and history.</P>
<HR NOSHADE>

<H2>Internet Basics</H2>

<P CLASS="intro">The Internet has grown from a military research project in the late 1960s to a global
network of computers today. The number of Internet users around the globe is expected to reach over 1 billion
by the year 2005. Offering everything from e-mail to information to commerce, the Internet brings users an
unprecedented way to communicate and exchange data. Constructed of thousands of networks and computers
around the world, the Internet connects organizations, governments, businesses, and individuals</P>

<H3>Types of Connections</H3>

<P CLASS="content">Users connect to the Internet through a variety of sources. Individuals can connect
through a modem and a phone line, cable, or satellite. If you use a modem to connect to the Internet, you
typically use a dial-up service, called an Internet Service Provider, or a commercial service, such as America
Online. You can also use cable TV companies to connect to the Internet through a cable modem, or you can
connect through digital phone lines, such as ISDN (Integrated Services Digital Network) and DSL (Digital
Subscriber Line).</P>
```

Welcome to my Web site. I'll show you how you can use HTML to create your own Web pages.

But first, let's start out with a little background and history.

Internet Basics

The Internet has grown from a military research project in the late 1960s to a global network of computers today. The number of Internet users around the globe is expected to reach over 1 billion by the year 2005. Offering everything from e-mail to information to commerce, the Internet brings users an unprecedented way to communicate and exchange data. Constructed of thousands of networks and computers around the world, the Internet connects organizations, governments, businesses, and individuals

Types of Connections

Users connect to the Internet through a variety of sources. Individuals can connect through a modem and a phone line, cable, or satellite. If you use a modem to connect to the Internet, you typically use a dial-up service, called an Internet Service Provider, or a commercial service, such as America Online. You can also use cable TV companies to connect to the Internet through a cable modem, or you can connect through digital phone lines, such as ISDN (Integrated Services Digital Network) and DSL (Digital Subscriber Line).

ASSIGN A CLASS

1 Open the HTML document and click in the tag to which you want to assign a class.

2 Type **CLASS="?"**, replacing the *?* with the class name.

The Web browser reads the instructions for the formatting and displays the properties you specified for the class.

What is a generic class?

You can use a generic class to format two or more different elements. For example, you might use a generic class to format both paragraphs and headings in a document, even though both elements use different tags. When defining a generic class, simply type a period followed by the class name, such as `.mytext`. When applying the class, use the class name, such as `<P CLASS="mytext">` or `<H2 CLASS="mytext">`.

How does inheritance work with classes?

When you apply a class, it inherits all the formatting that the class does not specifically override. For example, perhaps your HTML document contains three types of paragraphs. An introduction paragraph, a content paragraph, and a summary paragraph, and you want each to exhibit a slightly different appearance, yet all use the same font and size. You can use style rules to differentiate the changes in each, yet leave the font and size the same as defined in the `<P>` tag. Each class inherits the formatting of the `<P>` tag, but includes any overriding formatting, such as a change in bold or italics, or color.

Apply a Style with the DIV Tag

You can apply styles to different areas, or sections, of your Web page using the <DIV> tag. You can set up the <DIV> tag in your external or internal style sheet, and then apply it in your HTML document. When you apply styles with the <DIV> tag, the browser overrides the existing formatting for that particular section and replaces it with the style you specify.

You can use the <DIV> tag to group block-level elements, such as paragraphs and headings. When you apply the <DIV> tag, the Web browser inserts a blank line between the sections.

Apply a Style with the DIV Tag

SET UP THE DIV STYLE

① In your external or internal style sheet, type **DIV.?**, replacing the *?* with the name you want to assign the DIV style.

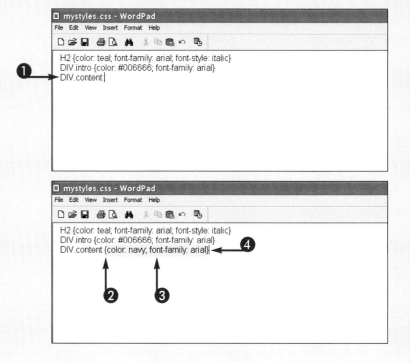

② Type {.

③ Type the properties and values for the DIV style.

If you intend to type more than one property, use a semicolon to separate properties.

Note: *See Chapter 6 to learn more about writing formatting style rules.*

④ Type }.

The style rule is complete.

If you are editing an external style sheet, save the sheet.

```
<HR NOSHADE>

<DIV CLASS="intro">
<H2>Internet Basics</H2>

<P>The Internet has grown from a military research project in the late 1960s to a global network of computers
today. The number of Internet users around the globe is expected to reach over 1 billion by the year 2005.
Offering everything from e-mail to information to commerce, the Internet brings users an unprecedented way to
communicate and exchange data. Constructed of thousands of networks and computers around the world, the
Internet connects organizations, governments, businesses, and individuals</P>
</DIV>

<DIV CLASS="content">
<H3>Types of Connections</H3>

<P>Users connect to the Internet through a variety of sources. Individuals can connect through a modem and a
phone line, cable, or satellite. If you use a modem to connect to the Internet, you typically use a dial-up service,
called an Internet Service Provider, or a commercial service, such as America Online. You can also use cable
TV companies to connect to the Internet through a cable modem, or you can connect through digital phone lines,
such as ISDN (Integrated Services Digital Network) and DSL (Digital Subscriber Line). </P>

<H3>Connection Speeds</H3>
<P>Connection speeds play an important part in a user's Internet experience. Slower connections result in
slower file transfers and Web page viewing. Modem connections offer the slowest connection speeds to the
Internet, up to 56 Kbps (Kilobits per second), followed by ISDN connections at 64-128 Kbps. Cable modems
can achieve connection speeds of 3000 Kbps and more, while DSL offers speeds of 1000-9000 Kbps.</P>
</DIV>
```

❶ **❷** **❸**

Internet Basics

The Internet has grown from a military research project in the late 1960s to a global network of computers
today. The number of Internet users around the globe is expected to reach over 1 billion by the year 2005.
Offering everything from e-mail to information to commerce, the Internet brings users an unprecedented way to
communicate and exchange data. Constructed of thousands of networks and computers around the world, the
Internet connects organizations, governments, businesses, and individuals

Types of Connections

Users connect to the Internet through a variety of sources. Individuals can connect through a modem and a
phone line, cable, or satellite. If you use a modem to connect to the Internet, you typically use a dial-up service,
called an Internet Service Provider, or a commercial service, such as America Online. You can also use cable
TV companies to connect to the Internet through a cable modem, or you can connect through digital phone
lines, such as ISDN (Integrated Services Digital Network) and DSL (Digital Subscriber Line).

Connection Speeds

Connection speeds play an important part in a user's Internet experience. Slower connections result in slower
file transfers and Web page viewing. Modem connections offer the slowest connection speeds to the Internet,
up to 56 Kbps (Kilobits per second), followed by ISDN connections at 64-128 Kbps. Cable modems can
achieve connection speeds of 3000 Kbps and more, while DSL offers speeds of 1000-9000 Kbps.

APPLY THE DIV TAG

❶ In the HTML document, click in front of the section to which you want to assign a DIV tag and add a line.

❷ Type **< DIV CLASS="?" >**, replacing the ? with the DIV style name.

❸ Type **</DIV>** at the end of the section.

● The Web browser displays the properties you specified for that particular area of the page.

Note: *Be sure to save your HTML document before attempting to view the page in a browser window. You can click the Refresh button in your browser to see updated changes you make to your HTML document.*

How do I format part of a paragraph or other element?
You can use the <SPAN> tag to apply formatting to a portion of text in your HTML document. Unlike the <DIV> tag, the <SPAN> tag is an inline tag, which means it does not add blank lines in between elements. To apply a style using the <SPAN> tag, first define the class you want to assign:

```
<STYLE>
SPAN.companyname {FONT: bold "Helvetica"}
</STYLE>
```

When you want to apply the style rule, your coding might look like this:

```
<P><SPAN CLASS="companyname">
```

proofread all your text

SPAN.highlight { background: yellow}

Apply a Style Locally

You can apply a style to a single instance of a tag in your document. For example, perhaps you want to make one of your level 2 headings stand out differently on the page than the rest of the level 2 headings. The STYLE attribute allows you to apply formatting like a style sheet without having to create an actual style sheet yourself.

When you apply a style locally, it overrides any styles found on external or internal style sheets for the same tag. Applying styles locally works best for one-time changes. You should use regular style sheets to control formatting and layouts on your pages.

Apply a Style Locally

1 Click in the tag for the element you want to change and type **STYLE="?"**, replacing the *?* with the properties and values you want to assign.

If you intend to assign more than one property, separate the properties with a semicolon.

Note: See Chapter 6 to learn more about writing formatting style rules.

■ The Web browser displays the element with the formatting you specified.

```
<HTML>
<HEAD>
<TITLE>Larry's HTML Tutorials</TITLE>
<LINK REL="stylesheet" TYPE="text/css" HREF="mystyles.css">
</HEAD>

<BODY BGCOLOR="silver">

<H1 STYLE="font-family: arial; color: navy">Learning HTML</H1>
<HR NOSHADE>
<BR>
<BR>

<P>Welcome to my W      e. I'll show you how you can use HTML to create your own Web pages.</P>

<P>But first, let's start out with a little background and history.</P>
<HR NOSHADE>

<H2>Internet Basics</H2>

<P>The Internet has grown from a military research project in the late 1960s to a global network of computers
today. The number of Internet users around the globe is expected to reach over 1 billion by the year 2005.
Offering everything from e-mail to information to commerce, the Internet brings users an unprecedented way to
communicate and exchange data. Constructed of thousands of networks and computers around the world, the
Internet connects organizations, governments, businesses, and individuals</P>

<H3>Types of Connections</H3>
```

Learning HTML

Welcome to my Web site. I'll show you how you can use HTML to create your own Web pages.

But first, let's start out with a little background and history.

Internet Basics

The Internet has grown from a military research project in the late 1960s to a global network of computers today. The number of Internet users around the globe is expected to reach over 1 billion by the year 2005. Offering everything from e-mail to information to commerce, the Internet brings users an unprecedented way to communicate and exchange data. Constructed of thousands of networks and computers around the world, the Internet connects organizations, governments, businesses, and individuals

Types of Connections

Users connect to the Internet through a variety of sources. Individuals can connect through a modem and a phone line, cable,

Apply a Style Using the ID Attribute

You can use the ID attribute to assign a style rule to an individual Web page element. Instead of creating a style sheet first, then applying the styles to your document, you can use the ID attribute to assign a style name to a tag first and then define the rule in the style sheet.

IDs are like classes, except they are not associated with specific elements. If you want to assign a style rule to more than one element of the same tag, create a class instead. See the section, "Create a Class," to learn more.

Apply a Style Using the ID Attribute

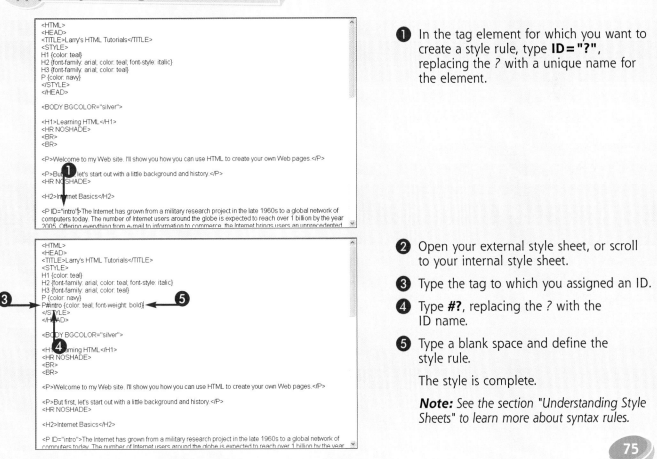

① In the tag element for which you want to create a style rule, type **ID="?"**, replacing the ? with a unique name for the element.

② Open your external style sheet, or scroll to your internal style sheet.

③ Type the tag to which you assigned an ID.

④ Type **#?**, replacing the ? with the ID name.

⑤ Type a blank space and define the style rule.

The style is complete.

Note: See the section "Understanding Style Sheets" to learn more about syntax rules.

Chapter 6

Formatting Text with Style Sheets

Ready to start formatting your Web page with style sheets? This chapter shows you how to apply formatting to your HTML elements using style sheet properties.

Add Bold
to Text

You can make Web page text bold using the `font-weight` property in a style rule. The bold value allows you to control the amount of boldness, ranging from a lighter value to a darker value. You can also specify the level of boldness using a multiple of 100, with 100 as the lightest and 900 as the darkest value.

Add Bold to Text

① Click inside the tag declaration and type **font-weight:**.

Note: To learn more about writing style sheets and rules, see Chapter 5.

② Type a space.

③ Type **bold**.

You can also specify a number value using a multiple of 100 to control the boldness level.

The Web browser bolds all the text to which the tag is applied.

● In this example, all the paragraph text is now bold.

Note: To learn more about how to link a style sheet to all the pages on your Web site, see Chapter 5.

Experts in gardening for over 40 years

We are located in beautiful Southern Illinois, just off of Route 13, south of Marion.

We offer the finest selection of plants and planting materials, and an award-winning gardening shop.

Stop by to see our 5 acres of nursery selections, including trees, shrubs, perennials, and seasonal plants. Our experienced staff is always available to assist you.

We are open 7 days a week, from 8-6 on Monday through Friday, 7-6 on Saturday, and 12-5 on Sunday. We sponser free gardening clinics every weekend throughout the spring and summer, plus autumn decorating clinics in September and October, and holiday decorating clinics during November and December. Click here for a complete schedule.

Our services include:

- Landscape design services
- Professional planting and yard maintenance services

Italicize Text

The `italic` value assigns an italic version of the font. If no italic version exists, `oblique` is the computer's attempt to turn the existing font into a slanted version to create italics. You can use the `normal` value to remove italics that may be inherited from previous paragraph elements.

You can use the `font-style` property to italicize Web page text. Italics are an easy way to add emphasis to text. You can choose from three values when italicizing text in a style sheet: `italic`, `oblique`, and `normal`.

Italicize Text

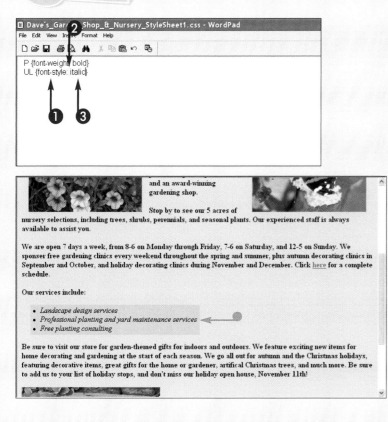

❶ Click inside the tag declaration and type **font-style:**.

Note: To learn more about writing style sheets and rules, see Chapter 5.

❷ Type a space.

❸ Type an italics value (**italic**, **oblique**, or **normal**).

The Web browser italicizes all the text to which the tag is applied.

● In this example, the unordered list text is italicized.

Indent Text

You can indent the first line in a paragraph using the `text-indent` property in a style rule. By default, the amount of indent is measured in pixels unless you specify another measurement.

You can also define a first line indent in millimeters (mm), centimeters (cm), inches (in), points (pt), picas (pc), x-height (ex), or em. You can also set the indent as a percentage of the overall text block width.

Indent Text

1 Click inside the tag declaration and type **text-indent: ?**, replacing *?* with the amount of space you want to indent, measured in pixels.

You can also set an indent size as a percentage of the text block width, or set a size measurement in millimeters (mm), centimeters (cm), inches (in), points (pt), picas (pc), x-height (ex), or em.

The Web browser indents the first line of all the text to which the tag is applied.

● In this example, all the <P> tags are indented.

Note: *To indent text with margins, see the section "Set Margins" later in this chapter.*

Change the Font Size

You can use the `font-size` property to change the font size for a document's text. Rather than going through your document and changing each instance of a tag, you can use the style sheet rule to change the font size for all uses of the tag in your document.

The `font-size` property allows you to set a font size using several different measurements. You can set the size in points, pixels, millimeters, centimeters, inches, picas, x-height (the height of the lowercase *x*), or em (the height of the current font). You can also specify the size as descriptive or relative. Descriptive includes the small, medium, or large values. Use the relative value to set a size percentage based on surrounding text.

Change the Font Size

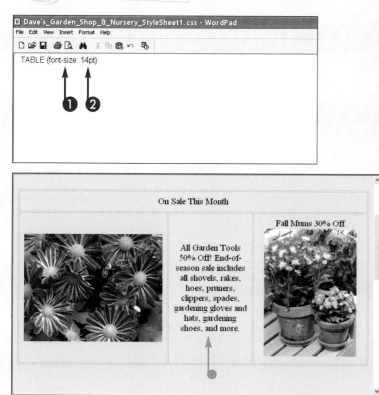

① Click inside the tag declaration and type **font-size:** and a space.

② Type a font size in points (pt), pixels (px), millimeters (mm), centimeters (cm), inches (in), picas (pc), x-height (ex), or em.

You can also type a descriptive (**xx-small**, **x-small**, **small**, **medium**, **large**, **x-large**, or **xx-large**) font size.

The Web browser uses the assigned font size for any text to which the tag is applied.

● In this example, all the table text reflects a larger font size assignment.

Note: *Learn how to create tables in Chapter 9.*

Change the Font

To change the font for your HTML text, you can use the `font-family` property. You can specify a font by name. Because not all fonts are available on all computers, you can designate a second or third font choice. This way, if the computer does not have the first choice installed, the browser tries to display the next choice instead.

For best results, try to stick with the more commonly used fonts, such as Arial, Verdana, Courier, and Times New Roman. You might also target other popular Windows fonts, including Impact and Comic Sans MS.

Change the Font

① Click inside the tag declaration and type **font-family:**.

Note: To learn more about writing style sheets and rules, see Chapter 5.

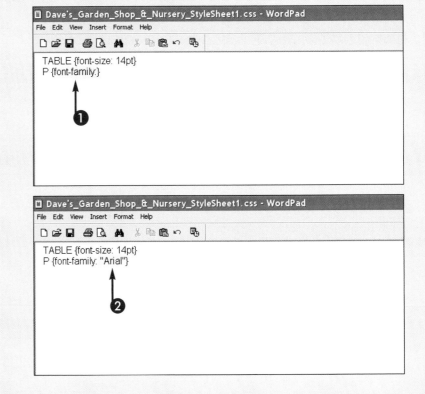

② Type a space and type **"?"**, replacing ? with the name of the font you want to use.

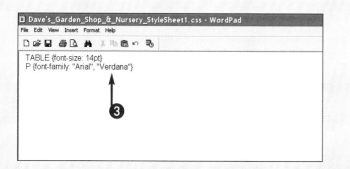

3 To designate a second font choice, type a comma, a space, and the second font name.

Be sure to enclose font names in double quotes.

You can repeat step **3** to assign additional fonts.

The Web browser uses the assigned font for any text to which the tag is applied.

● In this example, all the <P> tags reflect a new font assignment.

Can I change multiple font settings at the same time?
Yes. You can write a style rule that combines several font settings in one fell swoop using the font property. For example, you can designate the font, font size, and font style for a particular tag rather than write three different rules for the tag. Your combined rule might look like this:

```
P {font: italic 18pt "Times
New Roman", "Arial"}
```

Some browsers may require you to enter the properties in a particular order, such as font style before font size.

Is there a way to include a font with my page so users can see it even if they do not have the font installed?
Yes. You can embed the font in your Web page. If you embed the font, you must store it on the Web server, and it must use the .eot format, a requirement in Internet Explorer. You can use a special program, called WEFT, to convert an installed font into the .EOT format. Visit www.microsoft.com/ typography/web/embedding/weft/ to learn more. To embed the font in a style rule, follow this example:

```
@font-face {font-family:
"Sunnyside"; src:url(?.eot)}
```

Replace ? with the name of the embedded font.

Change the Text Case

You can use the `text-transform` property to change the text case for a tag. For example, you may want all <H1> text to appear in all capital letters. With the `text-transform` property, you can control how the browser displays the text regardless of how it was typed.

You can choose from four case values: `capitalize`, `uppercase`, `lowercase`, and `none`. Use the `capitalize` value if you want the first character of each word to appear capitalized. Use the `none` value to leave text as is. The `none` value cancels any case values the text may have inherited.

Change the Text Case

① Click inside the tag declaration and type **text-transform:** and a space.

② Type a text case value (**capitalize**, **uppercase**, **lowercase**, or **none**).

Note: To learn more about writing style sheets and rules, see Chapter 5.

The Web browser uses the assigned text case for any text to which the tag is applied.

● In this example, the <H2> tag is now displayed in uppercase letters.

☐ Dave's_Garden_Shop_&_Nursery_StyleSheet1.css - WordPad
File Edit View Insert Format Help

TABLE {font-size: 16pt; font-style: bold}
P {font-family: "Arial", "Verdana"}
H2 {text-transform: uppercase}

① **②**

Dave's Garden Shop & Nursery

| About Us | Garden Guide | Events | Links | Home |

DEALING WITH GARDEN PESTS

Is your garden infested? Tired of battling aphids and other pests? You can find plenty of insects that help to control bad bugs in your garden, and our garden shop can order them for you. For example, did you know that the Praying Mantis is one of the most useful insects to reside in your garden.

Ladybugs, also called lady beetles, are very beneficial group of insects for the garden. A single ladybug can consume as much as 5000 aphids in its lifetime. Ladybugs can be white, yellow, pink, orange, red or black, and typically have spots. Their bright color warns other insect predators of their distastefulness.

Change Text Alignment

You can control the horizontal positioning of block-level text in your page using the `text-align` property. Block-level text includes paragraphs, tables, and other elements that display a blank line before and after the element on the page. You can align text to the left or right, center the text, or create justified text. By default, most browsers align text to the left unless instructed otherwise.

Change Text Alignment

Dave's_Garden_Shop_&_Nursery_StyleSheet1.css - WordPad

File Edit View Insert Format Help

```
TABLE {font-size: 16pt; font-style: bold}
P {font-family: "Arial", "Verdana"}
H3 {text-align: center}
```

① ②

① Click inside the tag declaration and type **text-align:** and a space.

② Type an alignment (**left**, **center**, **right**, or **justify**).

Note: To learn more about writing style sheets and rules, see Chapter 5.

The Web browser uses the assigned alignment for any text to which the tag is applied.

● In this example, the <H3> tags are centered.

Dave's Garden Shop & Nursery

| About Us | Garden Guide | Events | Links | Home |

Dealing with Garden Pests

Is your garden infested? Tired of battling aphids and other pests? You can find plenty of insects that help to control bad bugs in your garden, and our garden shop can order them for you. For example, did you know that the Praying Mantis is one of the most useful insects to reside in your garden.

Ladybugs ⟵

Ladybugs, also called lady beetles, are very beneficial group of insects for the garden. A single ladybug can consume as much as 5000 aphids in its lifetime. Ladybugs can be white, yellow, pink, orange, red or black, and typically have spots. Their bright color warns other insect predators of their distastefulness.

Praying Mantis ⟵

The praying mantis is a remarkable insect in appearance, with a long torso and front legs that appear folded as if "in prayer." The mantis is carnivorous, eating other insects. Although the mantis has wings, it prefers to stand still in one spot and wait for unsuspecting prey to come along, in which case, the mantis immediately

Control Line Spacing

You can use the `line-height` property to adjust the spacing between lines of text. Also called leading, line spacing can make your Web page text easier to read. The line spacing value is specified as a multiple of the height of the element's font. For example, a line height value of 2.0 multiplies the current font height by 2.

You can also set the line spacing using a percentage of the font size, such as 50%, or an absolute value measured in pixels (px), points (pt), or another measurement.

Control Line Spacing

1. Click inside the tag declaration and type **line-height:** and a space.

2. Type a value for the spacing.

   For example, you can type **2.0** to multiply the spacing two times the current font height.

   You can also set a percentage or an absolute value for the spacing.

   Note: *To learn more about writing style sheets and rules, see Chapter 5.*

   The Web browser uses the assigned spacing for any text to which the tag is applied.

   In this example, the <P> tags all display extra line spacing.

Dave's_Garden_Shop_&_Nursery_StyleSheet1.css - WordPad

File Edit View Insert Format Help

```
H3 {text-align: center}
P {line-height: 2.0}
```

1   2

Dealing with Garden Pests

Is your garden infested? Tired of battling aphids and other pests? You can find plenty of insects that help to control bad bugs in your garden, and our garden shop can order them for you. For example, did you know that the Praying Mantis is one of the most useful insects to reside in your garden.

Ladybugs

Ladybugs, also called lady beetles, are very beneficial group of insects for the garden. A single ladybug can consume as much as 5000 aphids in its lifetime. Ladybugs can be white, yellow, pink, orange, red or black, and typically have spots. Their bright color warns other insect predators of their distastefulness.

Praying Mantis

The praying mantis is a remarkable insect in appearance, with a long torso and front legs that appear folded as if "in prayer." The mantis is carnivorous, eating other insects. Although the mantis has wings, it prefers to stand still in one spot and wait for unsuspecting prey to come along, in which case, the mantis immediately springs to action. The mantis is one of few insects fast

Set Margins

You can control the margins of your Web page elements using the margin properties. You can set margin values for the top, bottom, left, and right margins around a Web page element.

You can set margin sizing using points (pt), pixels (px), millimeters (mm), centimeters (cm), inches (in), picas (pc), x-height (ex), or em.

Set Margins

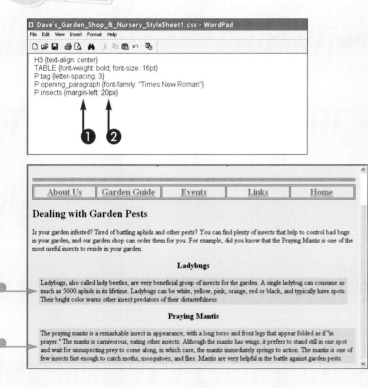

① Click inside the tag declaration and type **margin-?:** and a space, replacing *?* with the margin you want to adjust (**top**, **bottom**, **left**, or **right**).

② Type a value for the margin spacing.

The Web browser uses the assigned margins for the Web page element.

● In this example, margins are assigned to a paragraph class.

Note: *See Chapter 5 to learn more about creating classes in your style sheets.*

Add
Padding

You can use the **padding** property to add space around a Web page element. For example, you might add padding around an image, a table, or a heading.

You can specify padding in points (pt), pixels (px), millimeters (mm), centimeters (cm), inches (in), picas (pc), x-height (ex), or em.

Add Padding

① Click inside the tag declaration and type **padding:** and a space.

② Type a value for the spacing.

Note: To learn more about writing style sheets and rules, see Chapter 5.

The Web browser uses the assigned padding for the element to which the tag is applied.

● In this example, padding is added to a paragraph class.

Note: See Chapter 5 to learn more about creating classes in your style sheets.

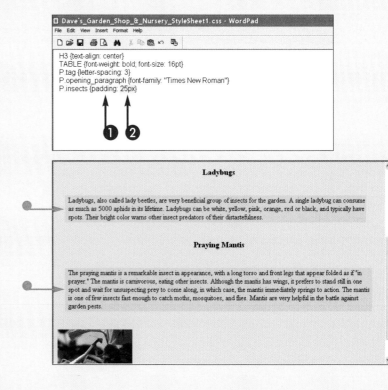

Add Color to Text

You can use the **color** property to change the color of text in your Web page. You can specify a color name from the 16 predefined colors or specify a color from the hexadecimal color palette.

You can also use the **color** property to change other Web page elements, such as tables, borders, and horizontal rules.

Add Color to Text

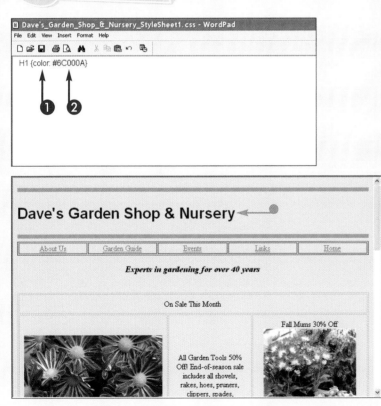

Dave's_Garden_Shop_&_Nursery_StyleSheet1.css - WordPad

File Edit View Insert Format Help

H1 {color: #6C000A}

1 **2**

Dave's Garden Shop & Nursery

| About Us | Garden Guide | Events | Links | Home |

Experts in gardening for over 40 years

On Sale This Month

Fall Mums 30% Off

All Garden Tools 50% Off! End-of-season sale includes all shovels, rakes, hoes, pruners, clippers, spades,

1 Click inside the tag declaration and type **color:** and a space.

2 Type a color name or hexadecimal value for the color you want to assign.

The Web browser uses the assigned color for the text to which the tag is applied.

● In this example, color is assigned to the <H1> tags.

Add a Border

You can add a border to a Web page element using the **border** property. A border can help separate the element from other Web page objects. You can specify a thickness value yourself, or you can specify one of three descriptive values: **thin, medium,** or **thick**.

You can specify a style for your border, choosing from **solid, double, groove, ridge, inset, outset, dotted,** or **dashed**. You can also assign a color value to a border.

Add a Border

① Click inside the tag declaration and type **border:** and a blank space.

② Type a thickness value in pixels, or specify a thickness (**thin, medium,** or **thick**).

> **Dave's_Garden_Shop_&_Nursery_StyleSheet1.css - WordPad**
> File   Edit   View   Insert   Format   Help
>
> P.opening_paragraph {border: medium|
>
> ①   ②

③ Type a space and type a border style (**solid, double, groove, ridge, inset, outset, dotted,** or **dashed**).

Note: If you do not set a border style with the border property, the browser will not display a border.

> **Dave's_Garden_Shop_&_Nursery_StyleSheet1.css - WordPad**
> File   Edit   View   Insert   Format   Help
>
> P.opening_paragraph {border: medium solid|
>
> ③

Dave's_Garden_Shop_&_Nursery_StyleSheet1.css - WordPad

File Edit View Insert Format Help

```
P.opening_paragraph {border: medium solid teal; padding:10px}
```

④

Dave's Garden Shop & Nursery

| About Us | Garden Guide | Events | Links | Home |

Dealing with Garden Pests

Is your garden infested? Tired of battling aphids and other pests? You can find plenty of insects that help to control bad bugs in your garden, and our garden shop can order them for you. For example, did you know that the Praying Mantis is one of the most useful insects to reside in your garden.

Ladybugs

Ladybugs, also called lady beetles, are very beneficial group of insects for the garden. A single ladybug can consume as much as 5000 aphids in its lifetime. Ladybugs can be white, yellow, pink, orange, red or black, and typically have spots. Their bright color warns other insect predators of their distastefulness.

Praying Mantis

---

④ To add a color to the border, type a space and the color value.

● In many instances, you will need to add some padding between the content and the border; you can use the `padding` property to do so.

Note: *See the section "Add Padding" to learn more.*

The Web browser uses the assigned border for the element to which the tag is applied.

● In this example, a border is added to a paragraph class.

Note: *See Chapter 5 to learn more about creating classes in your style sheets.*

Can I add a border to certain sides of an element instead of the entire element?
Yes. You can use the `border-left`, `border-right`, `border-top`, and `border-bottom` properties to designate which sides you want to add a border to. Your code may look like this:

`H3 {border-left: double 5px; border-right: double 5 px}`

In this example, a double border is added to the left and right sides of the heading.

Is there a way to remove all the borders on my page?
Yes. To remove borders, such as those that appear by default around linked images, you can use the `border` property and set the value to `none`. Your code looks similar to this:

`IMG {border: none}`

Control Element Position

You can position an element on your Web page absolutely or relatively. Typically, elements are positioned with respect to the surrounding elements, that is the element preceding and following the element in the document.

When you set an *absolute* position, you control the distance from the other elements, but setting an absolute position may cause other elements to shift on the page and overlap. When you set a *relative* position, you can move the element without moving surrounding elements.

Control Element Position

SET AN ABSOLUTE POSITION

① Click inside the tag declaration and type **position: absolute;**.

② Type the direction you want to move (**top**, **bottom**, **right**, or **left**) and a colon (:).

③ Type a space and type the absolute distance, in pixels, you want to move the element away from the surrounding elements.

To move the element in more than one direction, add another direction separated by a semicolon (;).

The Web browser displays the element in the new position.

● In this example, the <IMG> tag is positioned absolutely on the page, causing the <P> and <H3> tags to overlap it.

Note: *Learn how to add images in Chapter 7.*

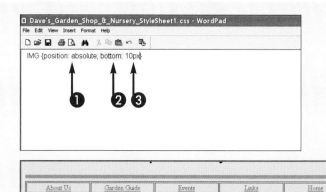

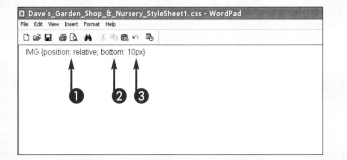

IMG {position: relative; bottom: 10px}

① ② ③

Dealing with Garden Pests

Is your garden infested? Tired of battling aphids and other pests? You can find plenty of insects that help to control bad bugs in your garden, and our garden shop can order them for you. For example, did you know that the Praying Mantis is one of the most useful insects to reside in your garden.

Ladybugs

Ladybugs, also called lady beetles, are very beneficial group of insects for the garden. A single ladybug can consume as much as 5000 aphids in its lifetime. Ladybugs can be white, yellow, pink, orange, red or black, and typically have spots. Their bright color warns other insect predators of their distastefulness.

Praying Mantis

The praying mantis is a remarkable insect in appearance, with a long torso and front legs that appear folded as if "in prayer."

SET A RELATIVE POSITION

① Click inside the tag declaration and type **position: relative;**.

② Type the direction you want to offset (**top**, **bottom**, **right**, or **left**) followed by a colon (:).

③ Type a space and type the distance, in pixels, you want to offset the element.

The Web browser displays the element in the new position.

● In this example, the <IMG> tag is positioned relatively on the page, and the <P> and <H3> tags flow with the image.

Note: *Learn how to add images in Chapter 7.*

Can I make an element stay fixed on the screen while the user scrolls?

Yes. You can keep an element stationary, or fixed. You might use this property to keep a navigation button or list in view at all times whether the user scrolls up or down the page. To apply the property, your style sheet rule might look similar to this:

```
#navigation {position:
fixed; left: 10px}
```

Warning: not all browsers support the fixed positioning property. You may prefer to use frames to keep content in view. See Chapter 10.

In what ways can a style sheet control the elements on my Web page?

Your Web page elements flow from one to the next based on the order in which they are entered. Much like a page layout program, CSS assigns each element its own space on the page, similar to an invisible box. As such, you can control the content inside the box, the area surrounding the content, the border, and the space around the border. You can position an element by leaving it in the original flow order, remove it from the flow and position it exactly (absolute positioning), or move it in respect to its original position in the flow (relative positioning).

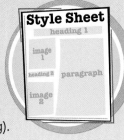

Wrap Text Around Elements

The **float** property does not work with elements for which you have assigned an absolute or fixed position.

You can use the **float** property to control how text wraps around the elements on your Web page. The **left** value controls the left side of an element, and the **right** value controls the right side of an element. To ensure proper text wrapping, the floating element should appear directly before the text you want to wrap.

Wrap Text Around Elements

① Click inside the tag declaration you want to control and type **float:** and a space.

② Type **left** to set the element to the left side of the text, or type **right** to set the element to the right side of the text.

The Web browser floats the element as directed.

● In this example, the <IMG> tag floats to the right of the text tags.

Note: Learn how to add images in Chapter 7.

□ Dave's_Garden_Shop_&_Nursery_StyleSheet1.css - WordPad

File Edit View Insert Format Help

IMG {float: right}

①②

| About Us | Garden Guide | Events | Links | Home |

Dealing with Garden Pests

Is your garden infested? Tired of battling aphids and other pests? You can find plenty of insects that help to control bad bugs in your garden, and our garden shop can order them for you. For example, did you know that the Praying Mantis is one of the most useful insects to reside in your garden.

Ladybugs

Ladybugs, also called lady beetles, are very beneficial group of insects for the garden. A single ladybug can consume as much as 5000 aphids in its lifetime. Ladybugs can be white, yellow, pink, orange, red or black, and typically have spots. Their bright color warns other insect predators of their distastefulness.

Praying Mantis

The praying mantis is a remarkable insect in appearance, with a long torso and front legs that appear folded as if "in prayer." The mantis is carnivorous, eating other insects. Although the mantis has wings, it prefers to stand still in one spot and wait for unsuspecting prey to come along, in which case, the mantis immediately springs to action. The mantis is one of few insects fast enough to catch moths, mosquitoes, and flies. Mantis are very helpful in the battle against garden pests.

Change Vertical Alignment

You can control the vertical positioning of elements on your page using the **vertical-align** property. You can choose from six different vertical alignments: **baseline, text-top, text-bottom, middle, top,** or **bottom.**

Change Vertical Alignment

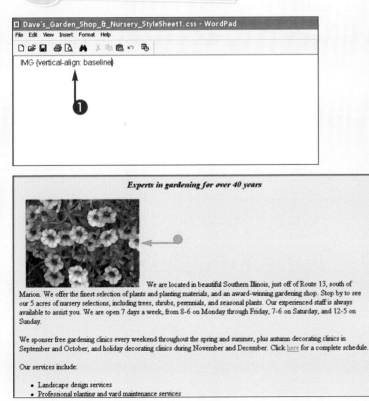

1 Click inside the tag declaration and type **vertical-align: ?**, replacing *?* with the vertical alignment option you want to assign (**baseline, text-top, text-bottom, middle, top,** or **bottom**).

The Web browser displays the element using the assigned vertical alignment.

● In this example, the <IMG> tag sits at the baseline of the text.

Note: *Learn how to add images in Chapter 7.*

Adding Images

Are you ready to add images to your Web page? Images include everything from photographs, logos, clip art, and other visual objects you can add to a Web page. This chapter shows you how to add and control images, including photographs, graphic files, and background images.

Understanding Web Page Images

You can use images in a variety of ways on your HTML pages. Images include everything from graphics and clip art, to photographs and other visual objects. Images can illustrate text, show a product, or act as navigational tools for a Web site. An important part of using images effectively on your own site is to understand how browsers display the images for others to view.

Image File Formats

Although there are numerous file types used for images, JPEG and GIF are the two most popular types used on the Web. Both formats are cross-platform and offer file compression. PNG is a newer arrival in the image file format world and is gaining popularity among Web developers. However, not all older browsers can support PNG.

JPEG

JPEG, or JPG, which stands for *Joint Photographic Experts Group*, supports 24-bit color, allowing for millions of colors. The JPEG format is commonly used with complex images, such as photos or graphics that use millions of colors and feature lots of detail. JPEG is not a good choice for simple artwork because it results in a larger overall file size, which in turn, takes longer to display on Web pages.

GIF

GIF, which stands for *Graphics Interchange Format*, supports up to 256 colors. The GIF format is more common with simple images, such as simple graphics utilizing basic shapes and lines, and logos. If your image or graphic contains few colors and not a lot of detail, GIF is a good file format choice.

PNG

The PNG format, which stands for *Portable Network Graphics*, offers rich color support and advanced compression schemes, and is a good choice for any kind of images, from graphics to photographs. PNG supports 24-bit color, like JPEG, but greater file compression. Choose PNG if your intended audience most likely uses a new browser version.

Downloading Considerations

Browsers must first download an image before users can view it on the Web page. Large images can take a long time to display, especially with slower Internet connection speeds. For this reason, you need to consider the overall file size of an image when deciding whether to add it to a Web page. Do not populate your page with many large pictures, or the download time will be excessive.

Optimize Images

Most image-editing programs allow you to make adjustments to the quality or resolution of the image to control file size. For best results, make sure your image file size does not exceed 60K, a good size for Web page images; if you use larger image files, many users will not wait for extended periods of time for the picture to download on-screen. You can also reduce the number of colors in an image to reduce the file size.

Insert an Image

You can use image files from a digital camera or scanner, or files you create with a graphics program. If you are not the original author of the image, you need permission to use the image before placing it on a Web site. (Using an image without permission violates copyright laws and exposes you to potential prosecution.) You can also find free clip art images on the Web.

CHOCOLATE IMAGE INSERT CANDY

You can add images to your Web page to add interest or illustrate a topic. For example, you can add a photograph or a graphic to your page. In HTML coding, images are inline elements, which means they appear within the body of the page along with text elements.

Insert an Image

INSERT A PHOTOGRAPH

1 Type **<IMG SRC="?">**, where you want to insert a photographic image, replacing the *?* with the full path to the file you want to insert.

```
<HTML>
<HEAD>
<TITLE>Dave's Garden Shop & Nursery</TITLE>
<BASE TARGET="_blank">
</HEAD>
<BODY BGCOLOR="#CCFFCC">

<H1 ALIGN="center"><FONT FACE="Arial">Dave's Garden Shop & Nursery</FONT></H1>
<HR>

<IMG SRC="Garden_Supplies.jpg">          ◀━━ 1

<P><B><I>Experts in gardening for over 40 years</B></I></P>

<P>We offer the finest selection of plants and planting materials, and an award-winning gardening shop. Stop by
to see our 5 acres of nursery selections, including trees, shrubs, perennials, and seasonal plants. Our experienced
staff is always available to assist you.</P>

<P>Be sure to visit our store for garden-themed gifts for indoors and out. We feature exciting new items for home
decorating and gardening each season.</P>

</BODY>

</HTML>
```

● The Web browser displays the image on the page.

Dave's Garden Shop & Nursery

Experts in gardening for over 40 years

We offer the finest selection of plants and planting materials, and an award-winning gardening shop. Stop by to see our 5 acres of nursery selections, including trees, shrubs, perennials, and seasonal plants. Our experienced staff is always available to assist you.

Be sure to visit our store for garden-themed gifts for indoors and out. We feature exciting new items for home decorating and gardening each season.

```
<!DOCTYPE HTML PUBLIC "-//W3C//DTD HTML 4.0 Tranistional//EN"
"http://www.w3.org/TR/REC-html40/loose.dtd">

<HTML>
<HEAD>
<TITLE>Kinkoph Designs</TITLE>
<META NAME="author" CONTENT="Greg Kinkoph">
<META NAME="description" CONTENT="Kinkoph Designs">
<META NAME="keywords" CONTENT="woodworking, custom woodworking, custom furniture, furniture
building">
<META NAME="copyright" CONTENT="2004">
</HEAD>
<BODY BGCOLOR="#FFFFCC">

<IMG SRC="Greg_Logo.gif">

<HR>
<P><FONT SIZE="5"><B><I>Custom woodworking and furniture designs to suit your home and office</FONT>
</B></I></P>

<IMG SRC="Sofa_Table.jpg" WIDTH="175" HEIGHT="175" HSPACE="20" ALIGN="center"> <IMG
SRC="Built_ins.jpg" WIDTH="175" HEIGHT="175" HSPACE="20" ALIGN="center"> <IMG
SRC="Corner_Table.jpg" WIDTH="175" HEIGHT="175" HSPACE="20" ALIGN="center">


<P><B>Whether you are looking for a unique furniture piece or a custom copy, we can create a timeless
classic you will treasure<BR>
```

**① **

INSERT A GRAPHIC FILE

① Type **<IMG SRC="?">**, where you want to insert a graphic, replacing the *?* with the full path to the file you want to insert.

Custom woodworking and furniture designs to suit your home and office

- The Web browser displays the graphic on the page.

What file types can I use for Web images?

The most common file type for photographs is JPG, or JPEG files. The most common type for simple graphics is GIF files. PNG is also gaining popularity as a cross-platform file type for image files; however, older browser programs do not support PNG. You can use an image editing or graphics program to save your images to specific file types. Most programs also offer options for optimizing the file size to create a smaller image file that downloads much faster. Consult your program's documentation to learn more.

When I insert an image, it appears too large on the Web page. How do I reduce its size?

You can use the Height and Width attributes within the <IMG> tag to set a specific display size for your image. For example, you may want to make your image 160 pixels wide and 210 pixels tall. See the section "Specify an Image Size" to learn more about applying these attributes to an image.

Specify an Image Size

If your image appears too big or too small on a Web page, you can use HTML coding to change the size with image attributes. You can set a size for the width and height of an image. The width and height is measured in pixels, or you can set the size as a percentage value of the overall window size.

Specify an Image Size

1 Click inside the <IMG> tag and type **WIDTH="?"**, replacing the ? with the width measurement you want to set.

```
<HTML>
<HEAD>
<TITLE>Dave's Garden Shop & Nursery</TITLE>
<BASE TARGET="_blank">
</HEAD>
<BODY BGCOLOR="#CCFFCC">

<H1 ALIGN="center"><FONT FACE="Arial">Dave's Garden Shop & Nursery</FONT></H1>
<HR>

<IMG SRC="Garden_Supplies.jpg" WIDTH="300">

<P><B><I>Experts in gardening for over 40 years</B></I></P>

<P>We offer the finest selection of plants and planting materials, and an award-winning gardening shop. Stop by to see our 5 acres of nursery selections, including trees, shrubs, perennials, and seasonal plants. Our experienced staff is always available to assist you.</P>

<P>Be sure to visit our store for garden-themed gifts for indoors and out. We feature exciting new items for home decorating and gardening each season.</P>

</BODY>

</HTML>
```

2 Type a blank space.

3 Type **HEIGHT="?"**, replacing the ? with the height measurement you want to set.

```
<HTML>
<HEAD>
<TITLE>Dave's Garden Shop & Nursery</TITLE>
<BASE TARGET="_blank">
</HEAD>
<BODY BGCOLOR="#CCFFCC">

<H1 ALIGN="center"><FONT FACE="Arial">Dave's Garden Shop & Nursery</FONT></H1>
<HR>

<IMG SRC="Garden_Supplies.jpg" WIDTH="300" HEIGHT="200">

<P><B><I>Experts in gardening for over 40 years</B></I></P>

<P>We offer the finest selection of plants and planting materials, and an award-winning gardening shop. Stop by to see our 5 acres of nursery selections, including trees, shrubs, perennials, and seasonal plants. Our experienced staff is always available to assist you.</P>

<P>Be sure to visit our store for garden-themed gifts for indoors and out. We feature exciting new items for home decorating and gardening each season.</P>

</BODY>

</HTML>
```

```
<HTML>
<HEAD>
<TITLE>Dave's Garden Shop & Nursery</TITLE>
<BASE TARGET="_blank">
</HEAD>
<BODY BGCOLOR="#CCFFCC">

<H1 ALIGN="center"><FONT FACE="Arial">Dave's Garden Shop & Nursery</FONT></H1>
<HR>

<IMG SRC="Garden_Supplies.jpg" WIDTH="50%" HEIGHT="30%">

<P><B><I>Experts in gardening for over 40 years</B></I></P>

<P>We offer the finest selection of plants and planting materials, and an award-winning gardening shop. Stop by to see our 5 acres of nursery selections, including trees, shrubs, perennials, and seasonal plants. Our experienced staff is always available to assist you.</P>

<P>Be sure to visit our store for garden-themed gifts for indoors and out. We feature exciting new items for home decorating and gardening each season.</P>

</BODY>

</HTML>
```

- You can also set the attribute value as a percentage. This tells the browser to display the image at a percentage of the browser window size.

  When setting a percentage value, be sure to add a percent (%) sign after the value.

Dave's Garden Shop & Nursery

Experts in gardening for over 40 years

We offer the finest selection of plants and planting materials, and an award-winning gardening shop. Stop by to see our 5 acres of nursery selections, including trees, shrubs, perennials, and seasonal plants. Our experienced staff is always available to assist you.

Be sure to visit our store for garden-themed gifts for indoors and out. We feature exciting new items for home decorating and gardening each season.

- The Web browser displays the specified image size on the page.

What size should I set for a Web page image?

The size of the image really depends on how you want to use it on the Web page. The average Web page measures approximately 600 pixels wide. For best results, set the image less than 40–50 percent of the page size, and keep the width and height values proportional. It is easier to scale a large image to a smaller size. If you make a small image too large, it appears grainy.

Is it better to resize an image in an editing program or use HTML coding?

Using an image editing or graphics program is the best way to resize an image for the Web. These types of programs give you complete control over an image, and allow you to set several optimizing options for an image so it is well suited for Web viewing.

Add Alternative Text

For users who do not have images turned on in their browser windows, you can add alternative text that identifies the images on your page. Alternative text, sometimes called placeholder text, helps describe the image, and is an important addition to your Web page markup.

Add Alternative Text

1 Click inside the <IMG> tag and type **ALT="?"**, replacing the *?* with the alternative text describing the image.

```
<HTML>
<HEAD>
<TITLE>Dave's Garden Shop & Nursery</TITLE>
<BASE TARGET="_blank">
</HEAD>
<BODY BGCOLOR="#CCFFCC">

<H1 ALIGN="center"><FONT FACE="Arial">Dave's Garden Shop & Nursery</FONT></H1>
<HR>

<IMG SRC="Garden_Supplies.jpg" WIDTH="300" HEIGHT="200" ALT="Image of Gardening Tool">

<P><B><I>Experts in gardening for over 40 years</B></I></P>

<P>We offer the finest selection of plants and planting materials, and an award-winning gardening shop. Stop by to see our 5 acres of nursery selections, including trees, shrubs, perennials, and seasonal plants. Our experienced staff is always available to assist you.</P>

<P>Be sure to visit our store for garden-themed gifts for indoors and out. We feature exciting new items for home decorating and gardening each season.</P>

</BODY>

</HTML>
```

● If the user's browser has downloaded images turned off, the Web browser displays the alternative text in lieu of an image.

Dave's Garden Shop & Nursery

Image of Gardening Tool

Experts in gardening for over 40 years

We offer the finest selection of plants and planting materials, and an award-winning gardening shop. Stop by to see our 5 acres of nursery selections, including trees, shrubs, perennials, and seasonal plants. Our experienced staff is always available to assist you.

Be sure to visit our store for garden-themed gifts for indoors and out. We feature exciting new items for home decorating and gardening each season.

Align an Image Horizontally

You can use the alignment attributes to control the horizontal positioning of an image on a page. The alignment attributes include **Left** and **Right**. By default, the image aligns to the left. The alignment attributes also control the way in which text wraps around the image.

You can also align an image vertically on a page. See the section "Align an Image Vertically" to learn more.

Align an Image Horizontally

```
<HTML>
<HEAD>
<TITLE>Dave's Garden Shop & Nursery</TITLE>
<BASE TARGET="_blank">
</HEAD>
<BODY BGCOLOR="#CCFFCC">

<H1 ALIGN="center"><FONT FACE="Arial">Dave's Garden Shop & Nursery</FONT></H1>
<HR>

<P><B><I>Experts in gardening for over 40 years</B></I></P>

<IMG SRC="Garden_Supplies.jpg" WIDTH="300" HEIGHT="200" ALT="Image of Gardening Tool"
ALIGN="Right">


</BODY>

</HTML>
```

1 Click inside the `<IMG>` tag and type **ALIGN="?"**, replacing the *?* with the alignment you want to apply, either **Left** or **Right**.

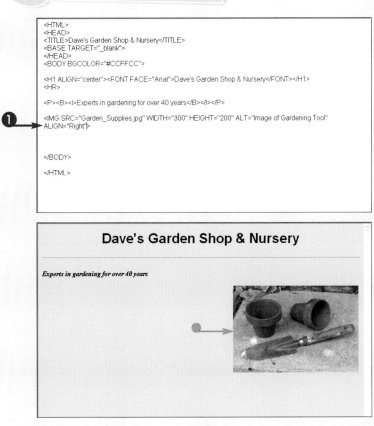

The Web browser aligns the image as specified.

● In this example the image is aligned to the right.

Note: For greater control over image alignment, consider placing your images in tables. Learn more about using tables in Chapter 9.

Align an Image Vertically

You can use the alignment attributes to control the vertical positioning of an image on a page. The alignment attributes include **Top**, **Middle**, and **Bottom**. These attributes are especially useful when you want to align the image with corresponding text on a page.

Align an Image Vertically

1 Click inside the <IMG> tag and type **ALIGN="?"**, replacing the *?* with the alignment you want to apply, either **Middle**, **Top**, or **Bottom**.

If the image shares the same line as text, you can use the alignment attribute to control the position of the image as it relates to the text.

```
<HTML>
<HEAD>
<TITLE>Dave's Garden Shop & Nursery</TITLE>
<BASE TARGET="_blank">
</HEAD>
<BODY BGCOLOR="#CCFFCC">

<H1 ALIGN="center"><FONT FACE="Arial">Dave's Garden Shop & Nursery</FONT></H1>
<HR>

<IMG SRC="Garden_Supplies.jpg" WIDTH="300" HEIGHT="200" ALT="Image of Gardening Tool"
ALIGN="Middle"><B><I><ALIGN="Center">   Experts in gardening for over 40 years</B></I>


</BODY>

</HTML>
```

The Web browser aligns the image as specified.

● In this example, the image is middle-aligned with existing text.

Note: *For greater control over image alignment, consider placing your images in tables. Learn more about using tables in Chapter 9.*

Dave's Garden Shop & Nursery

Experts in gardening for over 40 years

Center an Image

> You can center your image on the page using tags. Centering an image can give it more emphasis and help the image stand out from the text or other page elements.

Center an Image

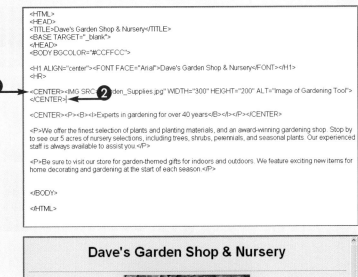

```
<HTML>
<HEAD>
<TITLE>Dave's Garden Shop & Nursery</TITLE>
<BASE TARGET="_blank">
</HEAD>
<BODY BGCOLOR="#CCFFCC">

<H1 ALIGN="center"><FONT FACE="Arial">Dave's Garden Shop & Nursery</FONT></H1>
<HR>

<CENTER><IMG SRC="Garden_Supplies.jpg" WIDTH="300" HEIGHT="200" ALT="Image of Gardening Tool">
</CENTER>

<CENTER><P><B><I>Experts in gardening for over 40 years</B></I></P></CENTER>

<P>We offer the finest selection of plants and planting materials, and an award-winning gardening shop. Stop by
to see our 5 acres of nursery selections, including trees, shrubs, perennials, and seasonal plants. Our experienced
staff is always available to assist you.</P>

<P>Be sure to visit our store for garden-themed gifts for indoors and outdoors. We feature exciting new items for
home decorating and gardening at the start of each season.</P>

</BODY>

</HTML>
```

1 Click in front of the `<IMG>` tag and type **`<CENTER>`**.

2 Click at the end of the image tag and type **`</CENTER>`**.

● The image appears centered on the Web page.

Dave's Garden Shop & Nursery

Experts in gardening for over 40 years

We offer the finest selection of plants and planting materials, and an award-winning gardening shop. Stop by to see our 5 acres of nursery selections, including trees, shrubs, perennials, and seasonal plants. Our experienced staff is always available to assist you.

Be sure to visit our store for garden-themed gifts for indoors and outdoors. We feature exciting new items for home decorating

Wrap Text Between Images

You can place two images side by side and wrap text between the two. To create this effect, you align one image to the left and the other to the right. Adjacent text flows between and around the images.

Wrap Text Between Images

❶ Insert the two images above the text you want to wrap.

❷ Click inside the first `<IMG>` tag and type **ALIGN = "Left"**.

❸ Click inside the second `<IMG>` tag and type **ALIGN = "Right"**.

```
<TITLE>Dave's Garden Shop & Nursery</TITLE>
<BASE TARGET="_blank">
</HEAD>
<BODY BGCOLOR="#CCFFCC">

<H1 ALIGN="center"><FONT FACE="Arial">Dave's Garden Shop & Nursery</FONT></H1>
<HR>

<CENTER><IMG SRC="Garden_Sup    .jpg" WIDTH="300" HEIGHT="200" ALT="Image of Gardening
Tool"></CENTER>

<CENTER><P><B><I>Experts in gardening for over 40 years</B></I></P></CENTER>

<IMG SRC="Million_Bells2.jpg" ALIGN="Left">
<IMG SRC="Butterfly3.jpg" ALIGN="Right">

<P>We offer the finest selection of plants and planting materials, and an award-winning gardening shop. Stop
by to see our 5 acres of nursery selections, including trees, shrubs, perennials, and seasonal plants. Our
experienced staff is always available to assist you.</P>

<P>Be sure to visit our store for garden-themed gifts for indoors and outdoors. We feature exciting new items
for home decorating and gardening at the start of each season.</P>


</BODY>

</HTML>
```

● The text wraps between the two images on the Web page.

Note: See the section "Add Space Around an Image" to learn how to add space between an image and surrounding text.

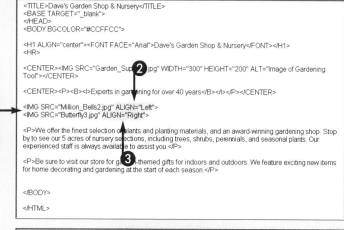

Experts in gardening for over 40 years

We offer the finest selection of plants and planting materials, and an award-winning gardening shop. Stop by to see our 5 acres of nursery selections, including trees, shrubs, perennials, and seasonal plants. Our experienced staff is always available to assist you.

Stop Text Wrap

You can stop text wrapping around your images using the line break tag along with the **Clear** attribute. When you stop text wrap, text returns to the default margins for the document page.

Stop Text Wrap

```
<TITLE>Dave's Garden Shop & Nursery</TITLE>
<BASE TARGET="_blank">
</HEAD>
<BODY BGCOLOR="#CCFFCC">

<H1 ALIGN="center"><FONT FACE="Arial">Dave's Garden Shop & Nursery</FONT></H1>
<HR>

<CENTER><IMG SRC="Garden_Supplies.jpg" WIDTH="300" HEIGHT="200" ALT="Image of Gardening
Tool"></CENTER>

<CENTER><P><B><I>Experts in gardening for over 40 years</B></I></P></CENTER>

<IMG SRC="Million_Bells2.jpg" ALIGN="Left">
<IMG SRC="Butterfly3.jpg" ALIGN="Right">

<P>We offer the finest selection of plants and planting materials, and an award-winning gardening shop. Stop
by to see our 5 acres of nursery selections, including trees, shrubs, perennials, and seasonal plants. Our
experienced staff is always available to assist you.</P><BR CLEAR="All">

<P>Be sure to visit our store for garden-themed gifts for indoors and outdoors. We feature exciting new items
for home decorating and gardening at the start of each season.</P>

</BODY>

</HTML>
```

1 Click where you want to end the text wrap and type **<BR CLEAR="?">**, replacing the *?* with the margin you want to clear, either **Left**, **Right**, or **All**.

The text wrapping ends at the selected point on the page.

● In this example, the next paragraph starts on a different line than the images.

Experts in gardening for over 40 years

We offer the finest selection of plants and planting materials, and an award-winning gardening shop. Stop by to see our 5 acres of nursery selections, including trees, shrubs, perennials, and seasonal plants. Our experienced staff is always available to assist you.

Be sure to visit our store for garden-themed gifts for indoors and outdoors. We feature exciting new items for home decorating and gardening at the start of each season.

Set an Image Border

You can add a border to an image to give it added emphasis or make the image more attractive on the page. You can define the thickness of the border, measured in pixels.

Set an Image Border

1 Click inside the `<IMG>` tag and type **BORDER="?"**, replacing the ? with the thickness value you want to apply.

To remove a border you no longer want, replace the ? with **0**.

```
<TITLE>Dave's Garden Shop & Nursery</TITLE>
<BASE TARGET="_blank">
</HEAD>
<BODY BGCOLOR="#CCFFCC">

<H1 ALIGN="center"><FONT FACE="Arial">Dave's Garden Shop & Nursery</FONT></H1>
<HR>

<CENTER><IMG SRC="Garden_Supplies.jpg" WIDTH="300" HEIGHT="200" ALT="Image of Gardening
Tool" BORDER="10"></CENTER>

<CENTER><P><B><I>Experts in gardening for over 40 years</B></I></P></CENTER>

<IMG SRC="Million_Bells2.jpg" ALIGN="Left">
<IMG SRC="Butterfly3.jpg" ALIGN="Right">

<P>We offer the finest selection of plants and planting materials, and an award-winning gardening shop. Stop
by to see our 5 acres of nursery selections, including trees, shrubs, perennials, and seasonal plants. Our
experienced staff is always available to assist you.</P><BR CLEAR="All">

<P>Be sure to visit our store for garden-themed gifts for indoors and outdoors. We feature exciting new items
for home decorating and gardening at the start of each season.</P>

</BODY>

</HTML>
```

- The Web browser displays a border around the image.

   Note: You can also set a color for a border. See Chapter 4 to learn more about color attributes.

Dave's Garden Shop & Nursery

Experts in gardening for over 40 years

 We offer the finest selection of plants and planting materials, and an award-winning gardening shop. Stop by to see our 5 acres of nursery selections, including trees, shrubs, perennials, and seasonal plants.

Add Space Around an Image

Most Web browsers display only a small amount of space between images and text. You can increase the amount of space, also called padding, to make the page more visually appealing and easier to read. You can use the **HSPACE** attribute to control horizontal padding to an image, which adds space to the left and right of an image. You can use the **VSPACE** attribute to add padding above and below an image.

The value used with the horizontal and vertical spacing attributes is measured in pixels. For example, a value of 25 adds 25 pixels.

Add Space Around an Image

```
<HTML>
<HEAD>
<TITLE>Dave's Garden Shop & Nursery</TITLE>
<BASE TARGET="_blank">
</HEAD>
<BODY BGCOLOR="#CCFFCC">

<H1 ALIGN="center"><FONT FACE="Arial">Dave's Garden Shop & Nursery</FONT></H1>
<HR>

<CENTER><IMG SRC="Garden_Supplies.jpg" WIDTH="300" HEIGHT="200" ALT="Image of Gardening
Tool" BORDER="10"></CENTER>

<CENTER><P><B><I>Experts in gardening for over 40 years</B></I></P></CENTER>

<IMG SRC="Million_Bells2.jpg" ALIGN="Left" HSPACE="15">
<IMG SRC="Butterfly3.jpg" ALIGN="Right" HSPACE="15">

<P>We offer the finest selection of plants and planting materials, and an award-winning gardening shop. Stop
by to see our 5 acres of nursery selections, including trees, shrubs, perennials, and seasonal plants. Our
experienced staff is always available to assist you.</P><BR CLEAR="All">
<BR>

<P>Be sure to visit our store for garden-themed gifts for indoors and outdoors. We feature exciting new items
for home decorating and gardening at the start of each season.</P>

</BODY>
```

1 Click inside the `<IMG>` tag and type **HSPACE = "?"** or **VSPACE = "?"**, replacing the *?* with the amount of space you want to insert.

You can add one or both attributes to an image.

If adding both attributes, separate them with a space in the HTML coding.

Experts in gardening for over 40 years

We offer the finest selection of plants and planting materials, and an award-winning gardening shop. Stop by to see our 5 acres of nursery selections, including trees, shrubs, perennials, and seasonal plants. Our experienced staff is always available to assist you.

Be sure to visit our store for garden-themed gifts for indoors and outdoors. We feature exciting new items for home decorating

● The Web browser displays the specified amount of space around the image.

Chapter 8

Adding Links

Are you ready to start adding links to your Web pages? This chapter shows you how to create all kinds of links in your HTML documents to allow users to jump to other pages or pages within your own site. You also learn how to add e-mail links and control the appearance of links.

INDENTIFICATION

VALID STANDARD PREFIX

HTTP://URL

TYPE: WEB PAGE

Mail To

Understanding Links

Hyperlinks, or *links* for short, are the heart and soul of Web pages. Links enable users to navigate from one topic to the next, and from one page to another. The user simply clicks the link and the browser immediately opens the designated page.

Types of Links

Links can be text or images. Most commonly, links appear as underlined text on a page. However, images also make good links. For example, graphical site maps and navigation bars that appear at the top or side of a page make it easy to link to other pages on the same Web site. When a user hovers his or her mouse pointer over a link, the pointer takes the shape of a pointing hand, indicating the presence of an active link.

Link to Other Web Pages

You can use links on your Web page to direct users to other pages on the Internet. For example, you might include a link on your company Web page to a local city directory detailing available activities and hotels in the area. Or you might add a link on a product page to the manufacturer's Web site.

Link to Other Pages on Your Site

If your Web site consists of more than one page, you can include links to other pages on the site. For example, your main page may provide links to pages about your business, products, and ordering information, and a map of your location.

Link to Other Areas on the Same Page

If your Web page is particularly long, you can provide links to different areas on the same page. For example, you might include links to each topic heading or photo on the page. This allows the user to jump right to the information he or she wants to view.

Absolute and Relative Links

You can use two types of links in your HTML documents: absolute and relative. *Absolute links* use a complete URL to point to a specific page on the Web. *Relative links* use shorthand to reference a page. You generally use relative links to reference documents on the same Web site.

Anchor Element

The HTML element you use to create a link is called an anchor element. Anchor elements are identified by the <A> and </A> tags. The HREF attribute works within the opening anchor tag to define the URL to which you want to link. You can learn more about using URLs in the next section, "Understanding URLs."

Understanding URLs

Every page on the Web has a unique address, called a URL. Short for *Uniform Resource Locator*, a URL identifies the domain name or host server where the page resides, and the directory path to the file. Absolute URLs link to a complete Web page address, whereas relative URLs link to Web pages relative to the current page in which the link is embedded.

HTTP Prefix

All URLs you type into an HTML document must include the standard HTTP prefix, such as http://www.myweb.com. The HTTP protocol identifies the URL as a Web page. Most browsers insert the prefix for you when you surf the Web, but when you design your own Web pages, you must include the full prefix to make the URL valid. If you are linking to a file transfer site (FTP) or e-mail address, you can use the FTP or MAILTO prefixes.

FTP or MAILTO Prefix

If you are linking to a file transfer site (FTP) or e-mail address, you can use the FTP or MAILTO prefixes instead of the HTTP prefix. For example, you might add a link to your e-mail address so that visitors can e-mail you about the Web site. You can also link to non-HTML resources, such as word processing documents and compressed files.

Host Name

Immediately following the identifying prefix is the name of the host server or domain name. Typically, host names are the name of the server or company storing your Web page files. Hosts can include commercial companies, educational institutions, and government agencies. In the URL http://www.mycompany. com, mycompany.com is the name of the domain.

Directory Path and Filename

If the page is stored in a directory on the server, the address generally includes a directory path to the file. For example, in the URL http://www.mycompany.com/webdocs/home.html, the slashes and directory names help define the path to the document file, home.html. In this example, the file is located within the webdocs directory. Directories act like folders found on your computer's hard disk drive.

Common URL Mistakes

One of the easiest ways to add an error to your Web page is to type the wrong URL for a link. A broken link that leads to an error page is very frustrating for users visiting your Web site. Be very careful to check over your URLs, paying careful attention to typos. You should also pay attention to the filenames and extensions. One misplaced letter in a filename can create a broken link.

Insert a Link to Another Page

You can create a link on your HTML document that, when clicked, takes the visitor to another page on the Web. You can link to a page on your own Web site, or to a page elsewhere on the Web.

In order to create a link, you must first know the URL of the page to which you want to link, such as `http://www.wiley.com`.

Insert a Link to Another Page

INSERT A TEXT LINK

1 Type the text you want to use as a link.

2 Type **<A HREF="?">** in front of the text, replacing *?* with the URL of the page to which you want to link.

3 Type **</A>** at the end of the link text.

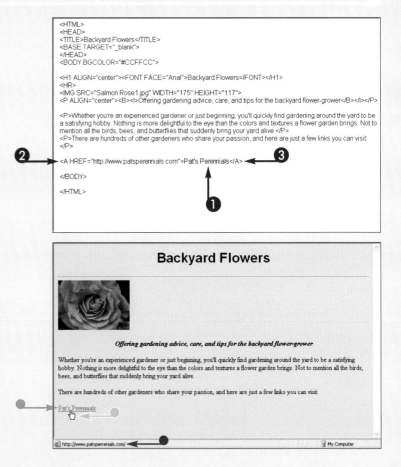

- The Web browser displays the text as an underlined link.

- Anytime the user moves the mouse pointer (⇗) over the link, it takes the shape of a hand pointer (☝), indicating a link.

- The URL for this link appears on the status bar.

```
<HTML>
<HEAD>
<TITLE>Backyard Flowers</TITLE>
<BASE TARGET="_blank">
</HEAD>
<BODY BGCOLOR="#CCFFCC">

<H1 ALIGN="center"><FONT FACE="Arial">Backyard Flowers</FONT></H1>
<HR>
<IMG SRC="Salmon Rose1.jpg" WIDTH="175" HEIGHT="117">
<P ALIGN="center"><B><I>Offering gardening advice, care, and tips for the backyard flower-grower</B></I></P>

<P>Whether you're an experienced gardener or just beginning, you'll quickly find gardening around the yard to be
a satisfying hobby. Nothing is more delightful to the eye than the colors and textures a flower garden brings. Not to
mention all the birds, bees, and butterflies that suddenly bring your yard alive </P>
<P>There are hundreds of other gardeners who share your passion, and here are just a few links you can visit
</P>

<A HREF="http://www.annasannuals.com"><IMG SRC="Anna Annual1.jpg" WIDTH="100" HEIGHT="75"></A>|

</BODY>

</HTML>
```

Backyard Flowers

Offering gardening advice, care, and tips for the backyard flower-grower

Whether you're an experienced gardener or just beginning, you'll quickly find gardening around the yard to be a satisfying hobby. Nothing is more delightful to the eye than the colors and textures a flower garden brings. Not to mention all the birds, bees, and butterflies that suddenly bring your yard alive.

There are hundreds of other gardeners who share your passion, and here are just a few links you can visit:

http://www.annasannuals.com/   My Computer

INSERT AN IMAGE LINK

1 Add the image you want to use as a link.

Note: See Chapter 5 to learn how to add images to a page.

2 Type **<A HREF="?">** in front of the image coding, replacing *?* with the URL of the page to which you want to link.

3 Type **</A>** at the end of the image coding.

● The Web browser displays the image as a link.

● Anytime the user moves the mouse pointer (⊠) over the link, it takes

the shape of a hand pointer (🖑), indicating a link.

● The URL for the link appears on the status bar.

How do I link to another page on my Web site?
You can link to another page on your site using a relative URL. Relative URLs allow you to simply list the name of the page file without needing to list the entire directory path, such as <A HREF="vacationphotos.html">. The page must be stored in the same directory or folder as the current page. If the page is stored in a subfolder, you must identify the name of the subfolder or subdirectory first, such as familyphotos/vacationphotos.html.

My link image includes a border. How do I remove the border?
When you turn an image into a link, a border automatically surrounds the image. To remove the border, type **BORDER="0"** in the <IMG> tag, such as <A HREF= http://www.mypage.com> <IMG SRC="vacation1.jpg" BORDER="0"></A>.

Insert a Link to a New Window

You use a **target** attribute within the link anchor element (**<A>**) to open links in new windows. By assigning the **target** the value **_blank**, it instructs the browser to keep your page open while opening a new unnamed window for the URL. To make all the links on your page open in new windows, you can use the **BASE** element. To learn more about how links and URLs work, see the sections at the beginning of this chapter.

You can add instructions to an HTML link that tell the browser to open the link page in a new browser window. You may add this instruction if you want to keep a window to your own site open so the user can easily return to your page.

Insert a Link to a New Window

LINK TO A NEW WINDOW

① Click within the <A> tag for the link you want to edit and type **TARGET="?"**, replacing *?* with a name for the new window.

To target a new, unnamed window, type **"_blank"**.

```
<HTML>
<HEAD>
<TITLE>Backyard Flowers</TITLE>
</HEAD>
<BODY BGCOLOR="#CCFFCC">

<H1 ALIGN="center"><FONT FACE="Arial">Backyard Flowers</FONT></H1>
<HR>
<IMG SRC="Salmon Rose1.jpg" WIDTH="175" HEIGHT="117">
<P ALIGN="center"><B><I>Offering gardening advice, care, and tips for the backyard flower-grower</B></I></P>

<P>Whether you're an experienced gardener or just beginning, you'll quickly find gardening around the yard to be
a satisfying hobby. Nothing is more delightful to the eye than the colors and textures a flower garden brings. Not to
mention all the birds, bees, and butterflies that suddenly bring your yard alive with life </P>
<P>There are hundreds of other gardeners who share your passion, and here are just a few links you can visit:
</P>

<A HREF="http://www.wiley.com" TARGET="_blank">Beginning gardening books from Wiley</A><BR>
<A HREF="http://www.annasannuals.com">Anna's Annuals</A><BR>
<A HREF="http://www.patsperrenials.com">Pat's Perrenials</A><BR>
<A HREF="http://www.gardensandmore.com">Gary's Gardening Guide</A><BR>

</BODY>

</HTML>
```

①

● When the link is clicked, a new browser window opens.

```
<HTML>
<HEAD>
<TITLE>Backyard Flowers</TITLE>
<BASE TARGET="_blank">
</HEAD>
<BODY BGCOLOR="#CCFFCC">

<H1 ALIGN="center"><FONT FACE="Arial">Backyard Flowers</FONT></H1>
<HR>
<IMG SRC="Salmon Rose1.jpg" WIDTH="175" HEIGHT="117">
<P ALIGN="center"><B><I>Offering gardening advice, care, and tips for the backyard flower-grower</B></I></P>

<P>Whether you're an experienced gardener or just beginning, you'll quickly find gardening around the yard to be
a satisfying hobby. Nothing is more delightful to the eye than the colors and textures a flower garden brings. Not to
mention all the birds, bees, and butterflies that suddenly bring your yard alive with life.</P>
<P>There are hundreds of other gardeners who share your passion, and here are just a few links you can visit:
</P>

<A HREF="http://www.wiley.com">Beginning gardening books from Wiley</A><BR>
<A HREF="http://www.annasannuals.com">Anna's Annuals</A><BR>
<A HREF="http://www.patsperrenials.com">Pat's Perrenials</A><BR>
<A HREF="http://www.gardensandmore.com">Gary's Gardening Guide</A><BR>

</BODY>

</HTML>
```
1

Backyard Flowers

Offering gardening advice, care, and tips for the backyard flower-grower

Whether you're an experienced gardener or just beginning, you'll quickly find gardening around the yard to be a satisfying hobby. Nothing is more delightful to the eye than the colors and textures a flower garden brings. Not to mention all the birds, bees, and butterflies that suddenly bring your yard alive.

There are hundreds of other gardeners who share your passion, and here are just a few links you can visit:

Beginning gardening books from Wiley
Anna's Annuals
Pat's Perrenials
Gary's Gardening Guide

MAKE ALL LINKS OPEN NEW WINDOWS

1 Click within the `<HEAD>` and `</HEAD>` tags and type **`<BASE TARGET="?">`**, replacing *?* with a name for the new window, such as **main**.

To target a new, unnamed window, type **`"_blank"`**.

● When a user clicks any of the links on the page, a new browser window opens.

Do I need to specify a name for the new window?
No. Rather than worry about what to name a new window, it is often easier to leave the window unnamed. Always use the `TARGET="_blank"` attribute if you do not want to create a window name.

Do I need to open new windows for every link?
No. If a new window opens every time a user clicks a link on your page, the user might become very irritated with the number of windows. For ease of use, keep the new windows to a minimum, and only when the links visit a page outside of your own Web site.

Insert a Link to an Area on the Same Page

You can add links to your page that, when clicked, take the user to another area on the same page. This is particularly useful for longer documents. For example, you can add links that take the user to different headings throughout your document.

The key to linking on the same page is assigning names to the various areas to which you want to link. You can do this with the **NAME** attribute. Keep your naming system simple, using only letters and numbers to name the sections throughout your document.

Insert a Link to an Area on the Same Page

NAME AN AREA

1 Click in front of the section of text to which you want to create a link and type **<A NAME="?">**, replacing the *?* with a unique name for the area.

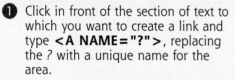

```
<H4><A NAME="Section3">Section. 3.</H4>
<H4>Clause 1: The Senate of the United States shall be composed of two Senators from each State, chosen
by the Legislature thereof, for six Years; and each Senator shall have one Vote.</H4>
<H4>Clause 2: Immediately after they shall be assembled in Consequence of the first Election, they shall be
divided as equally as may be into three Classes. The Seats of the Senators of the first Class shall be vacated
at the Expiration of the second Year, of the second Class at the Expiration of the fourth Year, and of the third
Class at the Expiration of the sixth Year, so that one third may be chosen every second Year; and if Vacancies
happen by Resignation, or otherwise, during the Recess of the Legislature of any State, the Executive thereof
may make temporary Appointments until the next Meeting of the Legislature, which shall then fill such
Vacancies.</H4>
<H4>Clause 3: No Person shall be a Senator who shall not have attained to the Age of thirty Years, and been
nine Years a Citizen of the United States, and who shall not, when elected, be an Inhabitant of that State for
which he shall be chosen.</H4>
<H4>Clause 4: The Vice President of the United States shall be President of the Senate, but shall have no
Vote, unless they be equally divided.</H4>
<H4>Clause 5: The Senate shall choose their other Officers, and also a President pro tempore, in the Absence
of the Vice President, or when he shall exercise the Office of President of the United States.</H4>
<H4>Clause 4: The Senate shall have the sole Power to try all Impeachments. When sitting for that Purpose,
they shall be on Oath or Affirmation. When the President of the United States is tried, the Chief Justice shall
preside: And no Person shall be convicted without the Concurrence of two thirds of the Members present.</H4>
<H4>Clause 7: Judgment in Cases of Impeachment shall not extend further than to removal from Office, and
disqualification to hold and enjoy any Office of honor, Trust or Profit under the United States: but the Party
convicted shall nevertheless be liable and subject to Indictment, Trial, Judgment and Punishment, according to
Law.</H4>
<H4>Section. 4.</H4>
```

2 Type **</A>** at the end of the section.

```
<H4><A NAME="Section3"></A>Section. 3.</H4>
<H4>Clause 1: The Senate of the United States shall be composed of two Senators from each State, chosen
by the Legislature thereof, for six Years; and each Senator shall have one Vote.</H4>
<H4>Clause 2: Immediately after they shall be assembled in Consequence of the first Election, they shall be
divided as equally as may be into three Classes. The Seats of the Senators of the first Class shall be vacated
at the Expiration of the second Year, of the second Class at the Expiration of the fourth Year, and of the third
Class at the Expiration of the sixth Year, so that one third may be chosen every second Year; and if Vacancies
happen by Resignation, or otherwise, during the Recess of the Legislature of any State, the Executive thereof
may make temporary Appointments until the next Meeting of the Legislature, which shall then fill such
Vacancies.</H4>
<H4>Clause 3: No Person shall be a Senator who shall not have attained to the Age of thirty Years, and been
nine Years a Citizen of the United States, and who shall not, when elected, be an Inhabitant of that State for
which he shall be chosen.</H4>
<H4>Clause 4: The Vice President of the United States shall be President of the Senate, but shall have no
Vote, unless they be equally divided.</H4>
<H4>Clause 5: The Senate shall choose their other Officers, and also a President pro tempore, in the Absence
of the Vice President, or when he shall exercise the Office of President of the United States.</H4>
<H4>Clause 4: The Senate shall have the sole Power to try all Impeachments. When sitting for that Purpose,
they shall be on Oath or Affirmation. When the President of the United States is tried, the Chief Justice shall
preside: And no Person shall be convicted without the Concurrence of two thirds of the Members present.</H4>
<H4>Clause 7: Judgment in Cases of Impeachment shall not extend further than to removal from Office, and
disqualification to hold and enjoy any Office of honor, Trust or Profit under the United States: but the Party
convicted shall nevertheless be liable and subject to Indictment, Trial, Judgment and Punishment, according to
Law.</H4>
<H4>Section. 4.</H4>
```

```
<HTML>
<HEAD>
<TITLE>US History for Fun</TITLE>
</HEAD>
<BODY BGCOLOR="#FFCCFF">

<H1>THE UNITED STATES CONSTITUTION</H1>

<P><A HREF="#Section 1">Section 1</A></P>

<P><A HREF="#Section 2">Section 2</A></P>

<P><A HREF="#Section 3">Section 3</A></P>

<P>We the People of the United States, in Order to form a more perfect Union, establish Justice, insure
domestic Tranquility, provide for the common defense, promote the general Welfare, and secure the Blessings
of Liberty to ourselves and our Posterity, do ordain and establish this Constitution for the United States of
America.</P>


<H2>Article. I.</H2>

<H3><A NAME="Section 1"></A>Section 1.</H3>
<P>All legislative Powers herein granted shall be vested in a Congress of the United States, which shall consist
of a Senate and House of Representatives.</P>
```

THE UNITED STATES CONSTITUTION

Section 1

Section 2

Section 3

We the People of the United States, in Order to form a more perfect Union, establish Justice, insure domestic Tranquility,
provide for the common defense, promote the general Welfare, and secure the Blessings of Liberty to ourselves and our
Posterity, do ordain and establish this Constitution for the United States of America.

Article. I.

Section 1.

All legislative Powers herein granted shall be vested in a Congress of the United States, which shall consist of a Senate and
House of Representatives.

Section. 2.

Clause 1: The House of Representatives shall be composed of Members chosen every second Year by the People

CREATE A LINK TO THE AREA

1. In front of the text or image you want to turn into a link, type **<A HREF="#?">**, replacing *?* with a name of the section to which you want to link.

   Note: Be careful not to leave out the pound sign (#) when linking to other areas of a page.

2. Type **</A>** after the link text.

   Note: You can also use an image as a link. See the section "Insert a Link to Another Page" to learn more.

● When a user clicks the link, the browser scrolls to the designated section of the page.

Can I place a link at the bottom of my page that returns the user to the top of the page?

Yes. It is always a good idea to add links to the bottom of a long document page to help the user navigate to the top again. To create such a link, first name the top section of the page following the steps shown in this section. Then include link text that describes the link, such as Return to Top or Back to Top, and add a link that takes the user to the named section at the top of the document.

How do I link to a specific location on another page on my Web site?

You can use the same technique shown in this section to link to another page on your site. Make sure you name the spot on the other page using the <A NAME="?"> tag and attribute.

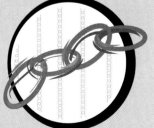

Link to an E-mail Address

You can add a link to your Web page that allows users to send you an e-mail message. Adding e-mail links is a good way to solicit feedback from your Web site visitors, as well as enable them to ask questions about you or your site.

Link to an E-mail Address

① Type the text you want to use as an e-mail link.

It is a good idea to mention the name or title of the person to whom you want the e-mails to go, or clearly indicate the link is an e-mail link.

② In front of the link text, type **<A HREF="mailto:?">**, replacing ? with the e-mail address you want to use.

③ Type **</A>** at the end of the link text.

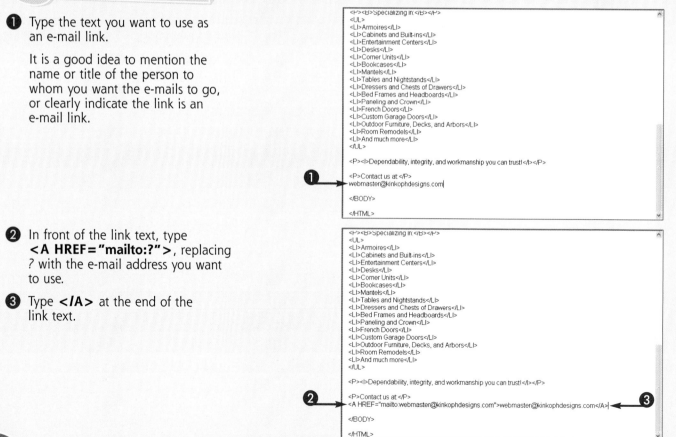

```
<P><B>Specializing in:</B></P>
<UL>
<LI>Armoires</LI>
<LI>Cabinets and Built-ins</LI>
<LI>Entertainment Centers</LI>
<LI>Desks</LI>
<LI>Corner Units</LI>
<LI>Bookcases</LI>
<LI>Mantels</LI>
<LI>Tables and Nightstands</LI>
<LI>Dressers and Chests of Drawers</LI>
<LI>Bed Frames and Headboards</LI>
<LI>Paneling and Crown</LI>
<LI>French Doors</LI>
<LI>Custom Garage Doors</LI>
<LI>Outdoor Furniture, Decks, and Arbors</LI>
<LI>Room Remodels</LI>
<LI>And much more</LI>
</UL>

<P><I>Dependability, integrity, and workmanship you can trust!</I></P>

<P>Contact us at </P>
webmaster@kinkophdesigns.com

</BODY>

</HTML>
```

```
<P><B>Specializing in:</B></P>
<UL>
<LI>Armoires</LI>
<LI>Cabinets and Built-ins</LI>
<LI>Entertainment Centers</LI>
<LI>Desks</LI>
<LI>Corner Units</LI>
<LI>Bookcases</LI>
<LI>Mantels</LI>
<LI>Tables and Nightstands</LI>
<LI>Dressers and Chests of Drawers</LI>
<LI>Bed Frames and Headboards</LI>
<LI>Paneling and Crown</LI>
<LI>French Doors</LI>
<LI>Custom Garage Doors</LI>
<LI>Outdoor Furniture, Decks, and Arbors</LI>
<LI>Room Remodels</LI>
<LI>And much more</LI>
</UL>

<P><I>Dependability, integrity, and workmanship you can trust!</I></P>

<P>Contact us at </P>
<A HREF="mailto:webmaster@kinkophdesigns.com">webmaster@kinkophdesigns.com</A>

</BODY>

</HTML>
```

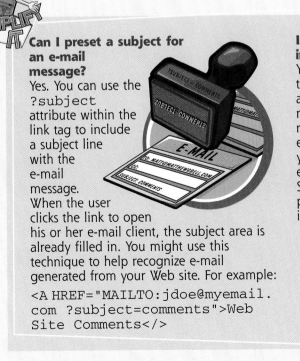

- The link appears in the Web browser.

- When the link is clicked, the user's e-mail editor opens with the To address filled in with the address you specified.

Can I preset a subject for an e-mail message?

Yes. You can use the `?subject` attribute within the link tag to include a subject line with the e-mail message. When the user clicks the link to open his or her e-mail client, the subject area is already filled in. You might use this technique to help recognize e-mail generated from your Web site. For example:

```
<A HREF="MAILTO:jdoe@myemail.
com ?subject=comments">Web
Site Comments</>
```

Is it safe to use my e-mail address in a link?

You should always use caution when thinking about placing a personal e-mail address online. E-mail addresses are notorious magnets for spamming. For this reason, you may want to create a special e-mail account just for your Web-generated e-mail messages. See your service provider for more information.

Chapter 9

Working with Tables

Are you looking for a method to organize data on a page? Need a way to control your page layout? Tables can help. This chapter shows you how to use tables as receptacles for different types of data.

Understanding Table Structure

Tables offer a unique way to hold data in a tabular format. With the advent of Web pages, developers quickly took advantage of table structures to help with complicated page layouts. Although CSS now allows users to create layouts without tables, HTML tables are still a popular way to organize and present Web page data and images.

Table Structure

Every table is built on a basic structure of a square containing four borders. Within the table, intersecting columns and rows create *cells* to hold data. Each cell is also surrounded by four borders. You can resize various borders in a table to increase the size of cells. Borders may or may not be visible in the table structure as it appears on the Web page.

Cell Spanning

Cells can span two or more columns or rows to form bigger containers for data. For example, a table may include a cell at the top that spans multiple columns across the table, or a cell that spans downward across several rows. When you span cells in a table, you add or delete interior cell walls to create a larger cell.

Traditional Tables

You can use traditional tables on a Web page to present data in a tabular format. For example, you might insert a table to hold a list of products and prices, or to display a roster of classes. One way to create a traditional table is to define a set width and depth for the table. When you define an exact size for a table, a user cannot resize the table; the table appears just as it was created.

Presentation Tables

You can use a presentation-style table to showcase your data more dynamically. Instead of defining an exact size, you can specify a table size using percentages. Whenever the user resizes his or her browser window, the table resizes as well. This allows for a more "liquid" layout. This type of table is good for page layouts as well as regular data tables.

Table Elements

The building blocks of HTML tables are the <TABLE>, <TR>, and <TD> codes. The <TABLE> element defines the table component. The <TR> tag defines a table row. The <TD> tag defines the table data, or cell content. In addition to these codes, you can assign table headers, captions, and column groups. You can also create tables within tables, called *nested tables*.

Preparing for a Table

Before you start the task of creating any kind of table, whether it is strictly for data or to control the page layout, stop and sketch out what you want the table to look like and what type of data you want each cell to hold. A little planning beforehand can help you build your table faster and more accurately using the HTML coding.

Add a Table

You can insert a table onto your page to organize data or control the entire page layout. Tables offer a manageable structure for creating a layout for your page. You can assign different page elements to different cells to control the positioning of elements on the page. Cells can hold text data, images, and other Web page elements.

Add a Table

① Type **<TABLE>** where you want to insert a table.

② Type **<TR>** to start the first row in the table.

To make the tag easier to distinguish between rows, type each row tag on a new line.

③ Type **<TD>** for the first cell you want to create.

④ Type the cell data.

Note: *If you want your first row to include column labels, you can use the <TH> tag instead of <TD>. See the section "Add Column Labels" to learn more.*

⑤ Type **</TD>** to complete the cell.

⑥ Repeat steps **3** to **5** to add additional cells.

To make it easier to distinguish between cells, you can place each cell on a new line in your HTML document.

⑦ Type **</TR>** at the end of the first row.

```
<HTML>
<HEAD>
<TITLE>Dave's Garden Shop & Nursery</TITLE>
<BASE TARGET="_blank">
</HEAD>
<BODY BGCOLOR="#CCFFCC">

<H1 ALIGN="center"><FONT FACE="Arial">Dave's Garden Shop & Nursery</FONT></H1>
<HR>

<CENTER><IMG SRC="Garden_Supplies.jpg" WIDTH="300" HEIGHT="200" ALT="Image of Gardening
Tool"></CENTER>

<P ALIGN="center"><B><I><FONT SIZE="5">Experts in gardening for over 40 years</FONT></B></I></P>

<IMG SRC="Million_Bells2.jpg" ALIGN="left" HSPACE="10"><IMG SRC="Butterfly3.jpg" ALIGN="right"
HSPACE="10">  We offer the finest selection of plants and planting materials, and an award-
winning gardening shop. Stop by to see our 5 acres of nursery selections, including trees, shrubs, perennials,
and seasonal plants. Our experienced staff is always available to assist you <BR CLEAR="all">
<BR>

Our Top-Selling Perennials:

<TABLE>       ①
<TR>          ②
<TD>Lavender  ④
```

```
winning gardening shop. Stop by to see our 5 acres of nursery selections, including trees, shrubs, perennials,
and seasonal plants. Our experienced staff is always available to assist you.<BR CLEAR="all">
<BR>

Our Top-Selling Perennials:

<TABLE>
<TR>
<TD>Lavender</TD>          ⑤
<TD>Daylily</TD>
<TD>Columbine</TD>         ⑥
<TD>Russian Sage</TD>
</TR>      ⑦

<P><I>Be sure to visit our store for garden-themed gifts for indoors and out. We feature exciting new items for
home decorating and gardening each season.</I></P>


</BODY>

</HTML>
```

```
winning gardening shop. Stop by to see our 5 acres of nursery selections, including trees, shrubs, perennials,
and seasonal plants. Our experienced staff is always available to assist you.<BR CLEAR="all">
<BR>

Our Top-Selling Perennials:

<TABLE>
<TR>
<TD>Lavender</TD>
<TD>Daylily</TD>
<TD>Columbine</TD>
<TD>Russian Sage</TD>
</TR>
<TR>
<TD>Daisy</TD>
<TD>Iris</TD>
<TD>Astilbe</TD>
<TD>Bee Balm</TD>
</TR>
<TR>
<TD>Hollyhock</TD>
<TD>Poppy</TD>
<TD>Primrose</TD>
<TD>Summer Phlox</TD>
</TR>
</TABLE>
```

⑧ Continue adding rows and cell data as needed.

⑨ Type **</TABLE>** at the end of the table data.

Note: The </TABLE> tag is not an optional tag. Netscape Navigator does not display a table without the tag.

Experts in gardening for over 40 years

We offer the finest selection of plants and planting materials, and an award-winning gardening shop. Stop by to see our 5 acres of nursery selections, including trees, shrubs, perennials, and seasonal plants. Our experienced staff is always available to assist you.

Our Top-Selling Perennials:
Lavender Daylily Columbine Russian Sage
Daisy   Iris   Astilbe   Bee Balm
Hollyhock Poppy Primrose   Summer Phlox

Be sure to visit our store for garden-themed gifts for indoors and out. We feature exciting new items for home decorating and gardening each season.

The Web browser displays the data in a tabular format.

● In this example, the table cells need some padding and spacing or borders displayed.

Note: See the sections "Assign a Table Border" and "Adjust Cell Padding and Spacing" to learn more.

How do I set an exact size for a table?
If you want your table to appear in a set width, you can measure how wide the table should be on the page, and then divide the value by how wide you want each column. For best results, do not set your table width any wider than 600 pixels to ensure the table is viewable at lower screen resolutions. See the section "Adjust the Table Size" to learn how to write HTML coding for an exact width using pixels or percentages.

What is the best procedure for building a table?
Before you type up your table coding, it is helpful to draw it out on paper first to organize the cell contents, designate column headers and rows, and determine a general layout and size of a table. When you are ready to enter the table coding, start with a skeleton of the page, typing just the tags to define the table structure, including the number of rows and columns. You can check the structure in a Web browser to see how it looks, and then return to your editor and start filling in the actual cell data.

Assign a Table Border

When you set a border thickness, it applies only to the outer edge of the table, not to the cells within the table. Border thickness is measured in pixels. Borders appear gray unless you specify a color. See the section "Adjust Cell Padding and Spacing" to learn how to control interior borders.

You can use table borders to make your cells easier to distinguish and give the table more structure on a page. A table border is simply a line that appears around a table as well as around each cell within the table. By default, a table does not have an actual border unless you specify one. You can use the BORDER attribute to turn table borders on or off.

Assign a Table Border

① In the <TABLE> tag, type **BORDER="?"**, replacing the ? with the value for the border thickness you want to set.

Note: See the section "Add a Table" to learn how to create a basic table.

```
Our Top-Selling Perennials:

<TABLE BORDER="5">
<TR>
<TD>Lavender</TD>
<TD>Daylily</TD>
<TD>Columbine</TD>
<TD>Russian Sage</TD>
</TR>
<TR>
<TD>Daisy</TD>
<TD>Iris</TD>
<TD>Astilbe</TD>
<TD>Bee Balm</TD>
</TR>
<TR>
<TD>Hollyhock</TD>
<TD>Poppy</TD>
<TD>Primrose</TD>
<TD>Summer Phlox</TD>
</TR>
</TABLE>

<P><I>Be sure to visit our store for garden-themed gifts for indoors and out. We feature exciting new items for home decorating and gardening each season.</I></P>
```

● To set a border color, type **BORDERCOLOR="?"** in the <TABLE> tag, replacing the ? with the color value you want to apply.

```
Our Top-Selling Perennials:

<TABLE BORDER="5" BORDERCOLOR="teal">
<TR>
<TD>Lavender</TD>
<TD>Daylily</TD>
<TD>Columbine</TD>
<TD>Russian Sage</TD>
</TR>
<TR>
<TD>Daisy</TD>
<TD>Iris</TD>
<TD>Astilbe</TD>
<TD>Bee Balm</TD>
</TR>
<TR>
<TD>Hollyhock</TD>
<TD>Poppy</TD>
<TD>Primrose</TD>
<TD>Summer Phlox</TD>
</TR>
</TABLE>

<P><I>Be sure to visit our store for garden-themed gifts for indoors and out. We feature exciting new items for home decorating and gardening each season.</I></P>
```

- In this example, the browser displays a table with a default gray border.

- In this example, the browser displays the same table with a color border.

Can I specify a border with a style sheet?

Yes. In your style sheet, type **TABLE** or **TD**, or the selector that denotes the portion of the table to which you want to apply a border. Then type {**BORDER:VALUE**}, with BORDER defining the border property and VALUE defining the border type. See Chapters 5 and 6 to learn more about applying style sheets to your Web pages.

Do I need to add borders if I am using a table as a layout for my Web page?

No. It's not a good idea to invoke the BORDER attribute for table layouts. With a layout, you want the table structure to define different sections of the page. If you assign a border, it adds a border to every section, which can distract from your page content.

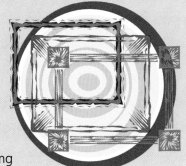

Adjust Cell Padding and Spacing

> You can use padding to add space between the border and the contents of a cell. You can use spacing to increase the border size or width between cells. Padding and spacing size is measured in pixels.

Adjust Cell Padding and Spacing

SET CELL PADDING

① In the <TABLE> tag, type **CELLPADDING="?"**, replacing the *?* with the pixel value you want to assign.

● The Web browser displays the designated amount of space between the contents and the cell borders.

Our Top-Selling Perennials:

```
<TABLE CELLPADDING="10">
<TR>
<TD>Lavender</TD>
<TD>Daylily</TD>
<TD>Columbine</TD>
<TD>Russian Sage</TD>
</TR>
<TR>
<TD>Daisy</TD>
<TD>Iris</TD>
<TD>Astilbe</TD>
<TD>Bee Balm</TD>
</TR>
<TR>
<TD>Hollyhock</TD>
<TD>Poppy</TD>
<TD>Primrose</TD>
<TD>Summer Phlox</TD>
</TR>
</TABLE>
```

<P><I>Be sure to visit our store for garden-themed gifts for indoors and out. We feature exciting new items for home decorating and gardening each season </I></P>

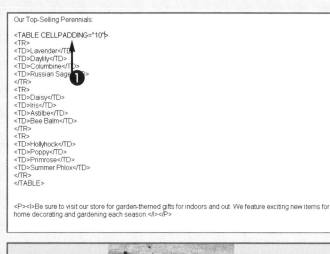

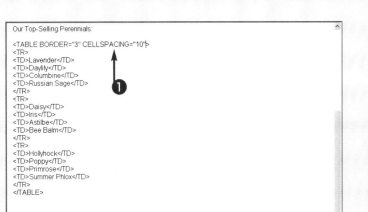

Our Top-Selling Perennials:

```
<TABLE BORDER="3" CELLSPACING="10">
<TR>
<TD>Lavender</TD>
<TD>Daylily</TD>
<TD>Columbine</TD>
<TD>Russian Sage</TD>
</TR>
<TR>
<TD>Daisy</TD>
<TD>Iris</TD>
<TD>Astilbe</TD>
<TD>Bee Balm</TD>
</TR>
<TR>
<TD>Hollyhock</TD>
<TD>Poppy</TD>
<TD>Primrose</TD>
<TD>Summer Phlox</TD>
</TR>
</TABLE>
```

`<P><I>`Be sure to visit our store for garden-themed gifts for indoors and out. We feature exciting new items for home decorating and gardening each season.`</I></P>`

Experts in gardening for over 40 years

We offer the finest selection of plants and planting materials, and an award-winning gardening shop. Stop by to see our 5 acres of nursery selections, including trees, shrubs, perennials, and seasonal plants. Our experienced staff is always available to assist you.

Our Top-Selling Perennials:

Lavender	Daylily	Columbine	Russian Sage
Daisy	Iris	Astilbe	Bee Balm
Hollyhock	Poppy	Primrose	Summer Phlox

SET CELL SPACING

1 In the `<TABLE>` tag, type **CELLSPACING="?"**, replace the *?* with the pixel value you want to assign.

● The Web browser displays the designated amount of space for the cell borders.

What happens if I set the spacing and padding values to 0?
If you set the CELLSPACING and CELLPADDING values to 0, the browser removes any spacing or padding between the cells. You may use this technique to make two images in two cells appear to be a part of one image. You can set the BORDER attribute to 0 as well to remove the border between cells.

How do I control the alignment of a table on a page?
You can control the positioning of a table on your Web page using the ALIGN attribute. You can use the ALIGN attribute to center a table, or align it to the right or left sides of the page. The ALIGN attribute also determines the way in which text wraps around your table element. For example, if you align the table to the right, text wraps around the left side of the table.

Adjust Cell Width and Height

You can control the width of a cell using the WIDTH attribute and the height of a cell using the HEIGHT attribute. Typically, the content of the cell determines the cell's width. For example, if the cell contains a long line of text, the cell appears wide enough in the browser window to hold all the text in the cell.

For greater control, you can specify a width based on a percentage of the browser window, or you can set an exact number of pixels. You can also control the depth of a cell using the HEIGHT attribute.

Adjust Cell Width and Height

SET CELL WIDTH

1 In the <TD> tag, type **WIDTH="?"**, replacing the *?* with the value or percentage you want to set for the cell.

To set the same cell width for the entire table, type the WIDTH attribute within the <TABLE> tag.

● The Web browser displays a set width for the cell, as well as all the other cells in the same column.

```
Our Top-Selling Perennials:

<TABLE BORDER="3">
<TR>
<TD WIDTH="100">Lavender</TD>
<TD>Daylily</TD>
<TD>Columbine</TD>
<TD>Russian Sage</TD>
</TR>
<TR>
<TD>Daisy</TD>
<TD>Iris</TD>
<TD>Astilbe</TD>
<TD>Bee Balm</TD>
</TR>
<TR>
<TD>Hollyhock</TD>
<TD>Poppy</TD>
<TD>Primrose</TD>
<TD>Summer Phlox</TD>
</TR>
</TABLE>

<P><I>Be sure to visit our store for garden-themed gifts for indoors and out. We feature exciting new items for home decorating and gardening each season.</I></P>
```

Experts in gardening for over 40 years

We offer the finest selection of plants and planting materials, and an award-winning gardening shop. Stop by to see our 5 acres of nursery selections, including trees, shrubs, perennials, and seasonal plants. Our experienced staff is always available to assist you.

Our Top-Selling Perennials:

Lavender	Daylily	Columbine	Russian Sage
Daisy	Iris	Astilbe	Bee Balm
Hollyhock	Poppy	Primrose	Summer Phlox

Be sure to visit our store for garden-themed gifts for indoors and out. We feature exciting new items for home decorating and gardening each season.

```
<TABLE BORDER="3">
<TR>
<TD WIDTH="100" HEIGHT="75">Lavender</TD>
<TD>Daylily</TD>
<TD>Columbine</TD>
<TD>Russian Sage</TD>
</TR>
<TR>
<TD>Daisy</TD>
<TD>Iris</TD>
<TD>Astilbe</TD>
<TD>Bee Balm</TD>
</TR>
<TR>
<TD>Hollyhock</TD>
<TD>Poppy</TD>
<TD>Primrose</TD>
<TD>Summer Phlox</TD>
</TR>
</TABLE>

<P><I>Be sure to visit our store for garden-themed gifts for indoors and out. We feature exciting new items for
home decorating and gardening each season.</I></P>
```

1

Experts in gardening for over 40 years

We offer the finest selection of plants and planting materials, and an award-winning gardening shop. Stop by to see our 5 acres of nursery selections, including trees, shrubs, perennials, and seasonal plants. Our experienced staff is always available to assist you.

Our Top-Selling Perennials:

Lavender	Daylily	Columbine	Russian Sage
Daisy	Iris	Astilbe	Bee Balm
Hollyhock	Poppy	Primrose	Summer Phlox

Be sure to visit our store for garden-themed gifts for indoors and out. We feature exciting new items for home decorating and gardening each season.

SET CELL HEIGHT

1 In the <TD> tag, type **HEIGHT="?"**, replacing the *?* with the pixel value or percentage you want to set for the cell.

To set the height for the entire table, type the HEIGHT attribute within the <TABLE> tag.

● The Web browser displays a set height for the cell, as well as all the other cells in the same row.

Which is more important, setting cell height or setting cell width?

Setting the cell width is more important than setting the cell height. The content of your cells typically define the height of the cell. You may never need to assign a cell height. Technically, the HEIGHT attribute is not normally associated with the <TABLE> tags. Some browsers do not support the attribute in tables, and as such, unpredictable results may occur when displaying the table in the browser window.

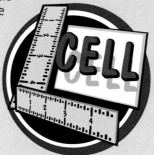

Can I set the width for a single cell and not affect the other cells?

When you change the width of a cell, all the cells in the same column adjust to the same width. If you want one cell to span across one or more columns, you can use another set of codes to control the individual cell width. See the section "Span Cells Across Columns and Rows" to learn more.

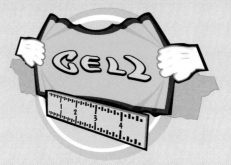

Add Column Labels

If you are building a table to populate with data, you can add labels, also called *headers*, to the top of each column to identify column contents. Any time you want to make your cell text bold and centered, you can use the <TH> tag. For example, if your table lists products and prices, column headers might include labels such as Product Number, Product Name, and Price. Column headers appear in bold type and are centered within each cell.

You can also give your table a title using the same <TH> tag. See the section "Add a Table Header" to learn more.

Add Column Labels

1 After the <TR> tag for the row you want to use as column labels, type **<TH>**.

Note: See the section "Add a Table" to learn how to create a basic table.

2 Type the first column label text.

3 Type **</TH>** at the end of the label.

4 Repeat steps **1** to **3** to add as many column labels as you need, ending the row with the **</TR>** tag.

 The Web browser displays the labels as column headers in the table.

```
<TABLE BORDER="4" BORDERCOLOR="maroon" CELLPADDING="10">
<TR>
<TH>Apple Variety</TH>
<TH>Price</TH>
<TH># of Apples</TH>
</TR>
<TR>
<TD>Jonathon Gold</TD>
<TD>$23.00</TD>
<TD>20-22 Apples</TD>
</TR>
<TR>
<TD>Red Delicious</TD>
<TD>$20.00</TD>
<TD>22-24 Apples</TD>
</TR>
<TR>
<TD>Fuji</TD>
<TD>$24.00</TD>
<TD>20-22 Apples</TD>
</TR>
<TR>
<TD>Honey Crisp</TD>
<TD>$25.00</TD>
<TD>18-20 Apples</TD>
</TR>
<TR>
<TD>Cortland</TD>
<TD>$21.00</TD>
```

Growing Peaches, Apples, Pears, and Pumpkins

Now taking orders for 2005 fall harvests

Fall Apple Pricing--

Apple Variety	Price	# of Apples
Jonathon Gold	$23.00	20-22 Apples
Red Delicious	$20.00	22-24 Apples
Fuji	$24.00	20-22 Apples
Honey Crisp	$25.00	18-20 Apples
Cortland	$21.00	20-22 Apples

Create Newspaper-Style Columns

You can use the table format to present columns of text on your Web page, much like a newspaper. For example, you may want to present your text in a two-column or three-column format. Paragraphs of text are contained within each column.

You can use the vertical alignment attribute to make each column align at the top of the table.

Create Newspaper-Style Columns

```
<HR NOSHADE SIZE="8">
<BR CLEAR="all">

<TABLE CELLPADDING="10">
<TR>
<TD VALIGN="top">Whether you are looking for a unique furniture piece or a custom copy, we can create a
timeless classic you will treasure for years to come. Offering old-world craftsmanship at a quality price, we build
a wide variety of beautiful furniture pieces, cabinetry, and built-ins to fit any home or office design and style.
</TD>
<TD VALIGN="top">At Kinkoph Designs, you'll experience dependability, integrity, and workmanship you can
trust. We do not send out a piece until it has met our rigid quality control checks. We also offer a lifetime
guarantee--unlike other furniture companies, we guarantee our pieces for the duration of your lifetime.
</TD>
<TD VALIGN="top">We offer a variety of building options suited to your pricing needs. We're happy to match
stains and paint from other pieces in your room, plus we offer a vast palette of our own custom shades. We also
sell unfinished furniture to allow our customers to paint or stain to fit their own decorating schemes.
</TD>
</TR>
</TABLE>

</BODY>

</HTML>
```

1 Within the `<TR>` and `</TR>` tags, type **<TD VALIGN="top">** to start the first column of text.

Note: *See the section "Add a Table" to learn how to create a basic table.*

2 Type your column text.

3 Type **</TD>** at the end of the text.

4 Repeat steps **2** and **3** to add more columns and text.

The Web browser displays the text as columns on the page.

Kinkoph Designs

Custom woodworking and furniture designs to suit your home and office.

Whether you are looking for a unique furniture piece or a custom copy, we can create a timeless classic you will treasure for years to come. Offering old-world craftsmanship at a quality price, we build a wide variety of beautiful furniture pieces, cabinetry, and built-ins to fit any home or office design and style.

At Kinkoph Designs, you'll experience dependability, integrity, and workmanship you can trust. We do not send out a piece until it has met our rigid quality control checks. We also offer a lifetime guarantee--unlike other furniture companies, we guarantee our pieces for the duration of your lifetime.

We offer a variety of building options suited to your pricing needs. We're happy to match stains and paint from other pieces in your room, plus we offer a vast palette of our own custom shades. We also sell unfinished furniture to allow our customers to paint or stain to fit their own decorating schemes.

Add a
Table Header

You can add a table header to the top of the table to give your table a title row. Text you type as a table header appears bold and centered. Table headers can help identify the content or purpose of a data table.

You can learn how to add captions, which sit outside the table borders, in the next section.

Add a Table Header

① Type **<TH>** at the top of the table.

Note: See the section "Add a Table" to learn how to create a basic table.

② Type the table header text.

③ Type **</TH>** at the end of the header text.

```
<TABLE BORDER="4" BORDERCOLOR="maroon" CELLPADDING="10">
<TH>Fall Apple Pricing</TH>
<TR>
<TH>Apple Variety</TH>
<TH>Price</TH>
<TH># of Apples</TH>
</TR>
<TR>
<TD>Jonathon Gold</TD>
<TD>$23.00</TD>
<TD>20-22 Apples</TD>
</TR>
<TR>
<TD>Red Delicious</TD>
<TD>$20.00</TD>
<TD>22-24 Apples</TD>
</TR>
<TR>
<TD>Fuji</TD>
<TD>$24.00</TD>
<TD>20-22 Apples</TD>
</TR>
<TR>
<TD>Honey Crisp</TD>
<TD>$25.00</TD>
<TD>18-20 Apples</TD>
</TR>
```

● The Web browser displays the text as a table header.

Growing Peaches, Apples, Pears, and Pumpkins

Now taking orders for 2005 fall harvests

Fall Apple Pricing		
Apple Variety	**Price**	**# of Apples**
Jonathon Gold	$23.00	20-22 Apples
Red Delicious	$20.00	22-24 Apples
Fuji	$24.00	20-22 Apples
Honey Crisp	$25.00	18-20 Apples
Cortland	$21.00	20-22 Apples

How to Order:

1. Specify an apple variety, pear variety, or pumpkin type and size

Add a Table Caption

> You can add a caption to your table to help users identify the information contained within the table. Table captions can appear at the top or bottom of the table. By default, captions appear above the table unless you specify another alignment attribute. Captions always appear as a separate line of text from the table.

Matt Zigaitis in victory lane after 3rd consecutive HTML 500 win

You can add formatting to your caption text using the HTML formatting tags. See Chapter 4 to learn more.

Add a Table Caption

```
<TABLE BORDER="4" BORDERCOLOR="maroon" CELLPADDING="10">
<CAPTION>Fall Apple Pricing</CAPTION>
<TR>
<TH>Apple Variety</TH>
<TH>Price</TH>
<TH># of Apples</TH>
</TR>
<TR>
<TD>Jonathon Gold</TD>
<TD>$23.00</TD>
<TD>20-22 Apples</TD>
</TR>
<TR>
<TD>Red Delicious</TD>
<TD>$20.00</TD>
<TD>22-24 Apples</TD>
</TR>
<TR>
<TD>Fuji</TD>
<TD>$24.00</TD>
<TD>20-22 Apples</TD>
</TR>
<TR>
<TD>Honey Crisp</TD>
<TD>$25.00</TD>
<TD>18-20 Apples</TD>
</TR>
```

Growing Peaches, Apples, Pears, and Pumpkins

Now taking orders for 2005 fall harvests

Fall Apple Pricing

Apple Variety	Price	# of Apples
Jonathon Gold	$23.00	20-22 Apples
Red Delicious	$20.00	22-24 Apples
Fuji	$24.00	20-22 Apples
Honey Crisp	$25.00	18-20 Apples
Cortland	$21.00	20-22 Apples

1 Add a new line directly below the `<TABLE>` tag.

Note: See the section "Add a Table" to learn how to create a basic table.

2 Type **`<CAPTION>`**.

To place the caption below the table, type **ALIGN = "bottom"** within the `<CAPTION>` tag.

3 Type the caption text.

4 Type **`</CAPTION>`** at the end of the caption text.

● The Web browser displays the caption above or below the table.

Control Which Borders to Display

This section includes a list of all external and internal border values for your quick reference.

Ordinarily, when you assign a border to a table, it surrounds the outside of the table as well as separates each cell. You can control which internal and external borders appear in your table using the **FRAME** attribute. For example, you can turn off the top and bottom borders of a cell, or display the entire right side of the table without a border. By controlling which borders appear, you can create a custom table.

Control Which Borders to Display

CONTROL EXTERNAL BORDERS

1 In the BORDER attribute for the table, type **FRAME="?"**, replacing the *?* with the value for the border display you want to set (**void**, **above**, **below**, **rhs**, **lhs**, **hsides**, **vsides**, or **border**).

The Web browser displays the table with the external borders you specified.

● In this example, the sides of the table are hidden.

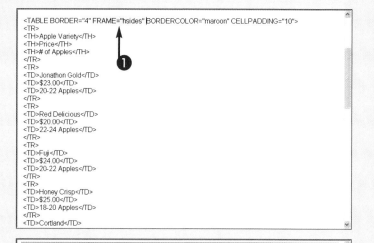

```
<TABLE BORDER="4" FRAME="hsides" BORDERCOLOR="maroon" CELLPADDING="10">
<TR>
<TH>Apple Variety</TH>
<TH>Price</TH>
<TH># of Apples</TH>
</TR>
<TR>
<TD>Jonathon Gold</TD>
<TD>$23.00</TD>
<TD>20-22 Apples</TD>
</TR>
<TR>
<TD>Red Delicious</TD>
<TD>$20.00</TD>
<TD>22-24 Apples</TD>
</TR>
<TR>
<TD>Fuji</TD>
<TD>$24.00</TD>
<TD>20-22 Apples</TD>
</TR>
<TR>
<TD>Honey Crisp</TD>
<TD>$25.00</TD>
<TD>18-20 Apples</TD>
</TR>
<TD>Cortland</TD>
```

Growing Peaches, Apples, Pears, and Pumpkins

Now taking orders for 2005 fall harvests

Apple Variety	Price	# of Apples
Jonathon Gold	$23.00	20-22 Apples
Red Delicious	$20.00	22-24 Apples
Fuji	$24.00	20-22 Apples
Honey Crisp	$25.00	18-20 Apples
Cortland	$21.00	20-22 Apples

How to Order:

```
<TABLE BORDER="4" RULES="cols" BORDERCOLOR="maroon" CELLPADDING="10">
<TR>
<TH>Apple Variety</TH>
<TH>Price</TH>
<TH># of Apples</TH>
</TR>
<TR>
<TD>Jonathon Gold</TD>
<TD>$23.00</TD>
<TD>20-22 Apples</TD>
</TR>
<TR>
<TD>Red Delicious</TD>
<TD>$20.00</TD>
<TD>22-24 Apples</TD>
</TR>
<TR>
<TD>Fuji</TD>
<TD>$24.00</TD>
<TD>20-22 Apples</TD>
</TR>
<TR>
<TD>Honey Crisp</TD>
<TD>$25.00</TD>
<TD>18-20 Apples</TD>
</TR>
<TD>Cortland</TD>
```

❶

Growing Peaches, Apples, Pears, and Pumpkins

Now taking orders for 2005 fall harvests

Apple Variety	Price	# of Apples
Jonathon Gold	$23.00	20-22 Apples
Red Delicious	$20.00	22-24 Apples
Fuji	$24.00	20-22 Apples
Honey Crisp	$25.00	18-20 Apples
Cortland	$21.00	20-22 Apples

How to Order:

1. Specify an apple variety, pear variety, or pumpkin type and size.

CONTROL INTERNAL BORDERS

❶ In the BORDER attribute for the table, type **RULES="?"**, replacing the *?* with the value for the border display you want to set (**none**, **cols**, **rows**, **groups**, or **all**).

The Web browser displays the table with the internal borders you specified.

● In this example, the inside row borders are hidden.

External Borders	
Value	**Display**
VOID	No external borders
ABOVE	A border above the table
BELOW	A border below the table
RHS	A border on the right side of the table
LHS	A border on the left side of the table
HSIDES	Borders on the top and bottom of the table
VSIDES	Borders on the left and right sides of the table
BORDER	Borders on every side of the table (default)

Internal Borders	
Value	**Display**
NONE	No internal borders
COLS	Borders between columns
ROWS	Borders between rows
GROUPS	Borders between column and row groups
ALL	Borders throughout the table cells (default)

Adjust the Table Size

When setting a size in pixels, set the value to 600 pixels or less to ensure the table fits on the screen. If you prefer a more flexible table, set the size in percentages. This allows the table to be resized along with any resizing of the browser window.

You can control the exact size of a table using the **WIDTH** and **HEIGHT** attributes in the **<TABLE>** tag. You can specify a table size in pixels or set the size as a percentage of the browser window.

Adjust the Table Size

SET A TABLE SIZE IN PIXELS

1 In the <TABLE> tag, type **WIDTH = "?"**, replacing the *?* with the pixel value you want to assign.

2 Type a space.

3 Type **HEIGHT = "?"**, replace the *?* with the pixel value you want to assign.

Note: *The HEIGHT attribute is not as well supported as the WIDTH attribute, and may not display properly on all browsers.*

● The Web browser displays the table in the specified size.

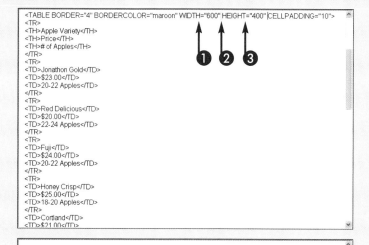

```
<TABLE BORDER="4" BORDERCOLOR="maroon" WIDTH="600" HEIGHT="400" CELLPADDING="10">
<TR>
<TH>Apple Variety</TH>
<TH>Price</TH>
<TH># of Apples</TH>
</TR>
<TR>
<TD>Jonathon Gold</TD>
<TD>$23.00</TD>
<TD>20-22 Apples</TD>
</TR>
<TR>
<TD>Red Delicious</TD>
<TD>$20.00</TD>
<TD>22-24 Apples</TD>
</TR>
<TR>
<TD>Fuji</TD>
<TD>$24.00</TD>
<TD>20-22 Apples</TD>
</TR>
<TR>
<TD>Honey Crisp</TD>
<TD>$25.00</TD>
<TD>18-20 Apples</TD>
</TR>
<TD>Cortland</TD>
<TD>$21.00</TD>
```

1 **2** **3**

Now taking orders for 2005 fall harvests

Apple Variety	Price	# of Apples
Jonathon Gold	$23.00	20-22 Apples
Red Delicious	$20.00	22-24 Apples
Fuji	$24.00	20-22 Apples
Honey Crisp	$25.00	18-20 Apples
Cortland	$21.00	20-22 Apples

```
<TABLE BORDER="4" BORDERCOLOR="maroon" WIDTH="100%" CELLPADDING="10">
<TR>
<TH>Apple Variety</TH>
<TH>Price</TH>
<TH># of Apples</TH>
</TR>
<TR>
<TD>Jonathon Gold</TD>
<TD>$23.00</TD>
<TD>20-22 Apples</TD>
</TR>
<TR>
<TD>Red Delicious</TD>
<TD>$20.00</TD>
<TD>22-24 Apples</TD>
</TR>
<TR>
<TD>Fuji</TD>
<TD>$24.00</TD>
<TD>20-22 Apples</TD>
</TR>
<TR>
<TD>Honey Crisp</TD>
<TD>$25.00</TD>
<TD>18-20 Apples</TD>
</TR>
<TD>Cortland</TD>
<TD>$21.00</TD>
```

1

Now taking orders for 2005 fall harvests

Apple Variety	Price	# of Apples
Jonathon Gold	$23.00	20-22 Apples
Red Delicious	$20.00	22-24 Apples
Fuji	$24.00	20-22 Apples
Honey Crisp	$25.00	18-20 Apples
Cortland	$21.00	20-22 Apples

How to Order:

1. Specify an apple variety, pear variety, or pumpkin type and size.
2. Fill out your shipping information.
3. Select a payment method.
4. Submit your order.
5. Receive a confirmation e-mail.

SET A TABLE SIZE AS A PERCENTAGE

1 In the `<TABLE>` tag, type **WIDTH="?"**, replace the *?* with the percentage value you want to assign.

Optionally, you can add a height setting if your table needs one by typing **HEIGHT="?"** in the `<TABLE>` tag to set a table height.

Note: *The HEIGHT attribute is not as well supported as the WIDTH attribute, and may not display properly on all browsers.*

● The Web browser displays the table in the specified size.

Is it possible to set a table too small for its contents?
No. If you do accidentally set a size too small for the contents, the browser ignores the measurements and tries to make the table fit as best it can. On the other hand, if you set a table too wide, users are forced to scroll to see parts of the table. For best results, do not make a table wider than 600 pixels.

What size does a browser set my table to if I do not specify an exact width?
If you do not set a width, the browser automatically determines the width by looking at the cell contents. It expands the table to fit the longest contents or the edge of the browser window, whichever is reached first. Cell text is stretched out until the first line break or end of the paragraph, which can make the table appear off balance. To exert control over the table size, you can set a width and add paragraph or line breaks to control the appearance of text within the cells.

Span Cells Across Columns and Rows

You can create a larger cell in your table by spanning the cell across two or more columns or rows. Spanning cells, also called merging cells, allows you to create unique cell structures within your table. For example, you might include a large cell across the top of a table to hold a heading or an image.

Span Cells Across Columns and Rows

SPAN CELLS ACROSS COLUMNS

① Click inside the cell tag you want to span.

② Type **COLSPAN="?"**, replacing the ? with the number of columns you want to span across.

```
<TABLE BORDER="4" BORDERCOLOR="maroon" WIDTH="600" CELLPADDING="10">
<TR>
<TH COLSPAN="3">Fall Apple Pricing</TH>
</TR>
<TR>
<TH>Apple Variety</TH>
<TH>Price</TH>
<TH># of Apples</TH>
</TR>
<TR>
<TD>Jonathon Gold</TD>
<TD>$23.00</TD>
<TD>20-22 Apples</TD>
</TR>
<TR>
<TD>Red Delicious</TD>
<TD>$20.00</TD>
<TD>22-24 Apples</TD>
</TR>
<TR>
<TD>Fuji</TD>
<TD>$24.00</TD>
<TD>20-22 Apples</TD>
</TR>
<TR>
<TD>Honey Crisp</TD>
<TD>$25.00</TD>
```

The Web browser displays the cell across the designated number of columns.

● In this example, a heading column spans across the top of the table.

Now taking orders for 2005 fall harvests

Fall Apple Pricing		
Apple Variety	**Price**	**# of Apples**
Jonathon Gold	$23.00	20-22 Apples
Red Delicious	$20.00	22-24 Apples
Fuji	$24.00	20-22 Apples
Honey Crisp	$25.00	18-20 Apples
Cortland	$21.00	20-22 Apples

How to Order:

1. Specify an apple variety, pear variety, or pumpkin type and size.
2. Fill out your shipping information.
3. Select a payment method.

```
<TABLE BORDER="4" BORDERCOLOR="maroon" WIDTH="600" CELLPADDING="10">
<TR>
<TH COLSPAN="4">Fall Apple Pricing</TH>
</TR>
<TR>
<TH ROWSPAN="6">Available Crop</TH>
<TH>Apple Variety</TH>
<TH>Price</TH>
<TH># of Apples</TH>
</TR>
<TR>
<TD>Jonathon Gold</TD>
<TD>$23.00</TD>
<TD>20-22 Apples</TD>
</TR>
<TR>
<TD>Red Delicious</TD>
<TD>$20.00</TD>
<TD>22-24 Apples</TD>
</TR>
<TR>
<TD>Fuji</TD>
<TD>$24.00</TD>
<TD>20-22 Apples</TD>
</TR>
<TR>
<TD>Honey Crisp</TD>
<TD>$25.00</TD>
```

SPAN CELLS ACROSS ROWS

1 Click inside the cell tag you want to span.

2 Type **ROWSPAN = "?"**, replacing the *?* with the number of rows you want to span across.

The Web browser displays the cell across the designated number of rows.

● In this example, a heading spans six rows down the side of the table.

Now taking orders for 2005 fall harvests

Fall Apple Pricing			
	Apple Variety	**Price**	**# of Apples**
Available Crop	Jonathon Gold	$23.00	20-22 Apples
	Red Delicious	$20.00	22-24 Apples
	Fuji	$24.00	20-22 Apples
	Honey Crisp	$25.00	18-20 Apples
	Cortland	$21.00	20-22 Apples

How to Order:

1. Specify an apple variety, pear variety, or pumpkin type and size.
2. Fill out your shipping information.
3. Select a payment method.

Can I span a cell across columns and rows at the same time?

Yes. If you add the COLSPAN and ROWSPAN attributes to the same row or header, you can make a cell span across and down in the table. Just remember to remove cells in the columns and rows into which you want to span the current cell.

How do I control table cell alignment?

You can control the alignment of data within your table cells using the ALIGN and VALIGN attributes. The ALIGN attribute controls horizontal alignment: left, center, and right. By default, all table data you enter into cells is left aligned. The VALIGN attribute controls vertical alignment: top, middle, bottom. By default, the table data is vertically aligned to appear in the middle of each cell. You can add alignment attributes to a single cell, a row, or all the data in the table.

Chapter 10

Working with Frames

Looking for a way to enhance your Web site layout? Frames can help you present multiple pages to your Web site visitors all on one screen. This chapter shows you how to create framesets and add frames to your Web site.

Understanding Frames

You can use frames to divide your Web page into sections and allow users to access different pages in your Web site from one screen. Although frames are not as widely used as they once were, they can still serve as a valuable tool to help you create a dynamic structure for your Web site.

Frame Basics

Browser windows typically hold a single frame to display an HTML document. If a page's content exceeds the size of the frame, scroll bars appear allowing the user to view different parts of the page. With multiple frames, the browser window displays several HTML documents at one time, each frame acting as a separate screen. Each frame can display its own scroll bars to allow users to view different portions of the Web page appearing within the frame.

Ways to Use Frames

You can find numerous uses for frames with a multi-page Web site. You can use frames to display a fixed page at the top of the screen and a scrollable page in the remainder of the screen. For example, you might use a navigation page at the top with links to pages on your site. When a user clicks a link in the top frame, the frame below displays the content. Or you might use side-by-side frames to display a picture in one frame and text in another.

Frame Advantages

When deciding whether to use frames in your Web site, take time to examine the pros and cons of frames. On the pro side, frames are really helpful with larger Web sites, especially when you want to keep certain information in view at all times. Frames offer a great way to display a navigation bar in one location without needing to include navigational links on every Web page in your site. Frames can make it easier for users to navigate a large Web site.

Frame Disadvantages

On the con side, users might not see your frame content as you envision; monitor resolution settings vary and what you think is the perfect size for a frame may not be so on another user's screen. Depending on the Web page, not all page content looks good in smaller frames. Although newer browsers support the use of frames, some older versions do not. You may need to design a non-frames version of your site to accommodate users without frame support. Frames can also complicate your HTML page coding, and when frames are not working properly, can cause user frustration. For example, you must test that the content of all frames in a three-frame set up work properly; improper loading may result in a user not being able to view the navigation tools in one frame resulting in a less than satisfactory visiting experience.

Framesets and Frames

You use several documents to create frames for your Web site. The frameset document, which is a part of HTML, defines the number and size of your frames. Within each frame you must target content, so you need separate HTML documents to appear within the frames. You can save the frameset document as a separate file and link other pages from your site to the frame structure. See the section "Create Frames" to learn how to make a frameset document.

Nesting and Inline Frames

If your Web site requires a more complex frame structure, you can nest a frameset within the original frameset. This gives you the flexibility of dividing a frame into more frames. You can also insert a single frame within any Web page on your site without needing to define a frameset document.

Create Frames

You can use the
`<FRAMESET>` and
`<FRAME>` tags to define
the frame structure. The
`<FRAMESET>` tag creates
a frameset, dividing the
window into sections,
while the `<FRAME>` tag
specifies which page
goes into which frame.
You can define the size
of each frame using an
absolute value, measured
in pixels, or a relative
value, measured as a
percentage.

You can use frames
to divide the Web browser
window into sections. This allows
you to display different pages in your
site on the screen at the same time. For
example, you might use one frame to
display a navigational page that helps
viewers access other parts of your site,
and then show the content of
a page in another frame.

Create Frames

① Create and save a new HTML
document, including only the
basic `<HTML>`, `<HEAD>`, and
`<TITLE>` tags.

Note: *See Chapter 2 to learn how
to create HTML documents.*

② Below the `</HEAD>` tag, type
`<FRAMESET` and a blank space.

③ Define the frameset to include two
or more rows or columns and specify
a size for the rows or columns.

To create frames in rows, type
`ROWS="?,?">`, replacing *?* with
the height of each row in your
frameset.

To create frames in columns, type
`COLS="?,?">`, replacing *?* with
the width of each column in your
frameset.

You can also set a row or column size
as a percentage by simply typing the
value followed by a percentage sign,
such as **30%**.

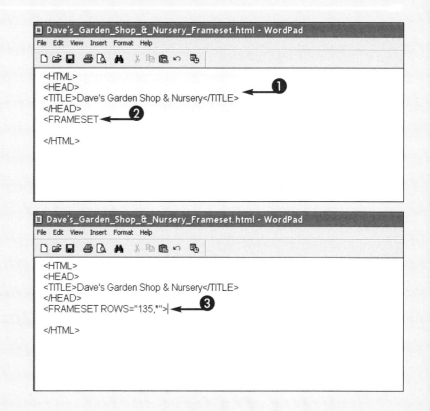

Dave's_Garden_Shop_&_Nursery_Frameset.html - WordPad

File   Edit   View   Insert   Format   Help

```
<HTML>
<HEAD>
<TITLE>Dave's Garden Shop & Nursery</TITLE>      ①
</HEAD>
<FRAMESET      ②

</HTML>
```

Dave's_Garden_Shop_&_Nursery_Frameset.html - WordPad

File   Edit   View   Insert   Format   Help

```
<HTML>
<HEAD>
<TITLE>Dave's Garden Shop & Nursery</TITLE>
</HEAD>
<FRAMESET ROWS="135,*">|      ③

</HTML>
```

```
Dave's_Garden_Shop_&_Nursery_Frameset.html - WordPad
File  Edit  View  Insert  Format  Help

<HTML>
<HEAD>
<TITLE>Dave's Garden Shop & Nursery</TITLE>
</HEAD>
<FRAMESET ROWS="135,*">
    <FRAME NAME="banner" SRC="Dave's_Garden_Shop_&_Nursery_Banner.html">
    <FRAME NAME="main" SRC="Dave's_Garden_Shop_&_Nursery_Main.html">
</FRAMESET>

</HTML>
```

Dave's Garden Shop & Nursery

Experts in gardening for over 40 years

We offer the finest selection of plants and planting materials, and an award-winning gardening shop. Stop by to see our 5 acres of nursery selections, including trees, shrubs, perennials, and seasonal plants.

④ Type **<FRAME NAME="?"**, replacing *?* with a name for the frame.

⑤ Type a space and **SRC="?">**, replacing *?* with the name and location of the Web page you want to appear in the frame.

⑥ Repeat steps **4** and **5** for each frame you specified in step **3**.

⑦ Type **</FRAMESET>**.

The Web browser displays the frames.

In this example, two frames appear in the browser window.

You can use a nested frameset to combine both rows and columns in a frameset.

Do I need to declare my frameset document somewhere on the Web page?

It is good practice to include a DOCTYPE declaration on your page. Frameset is a type of HTML document, and adding a statement specifying what version of HTML you are using can help identify the document type to others. Your DOCTYPE declaration might look like this:

```
<!DOCTYPE HTML PUBLIC "-//W3C/
DTD HTML 4.0 Frameset//EN"
```

```
http://www.w3.org/TR/
REC-html40/frameset.dtd>
```

See Chapter 2 to learn more about document declarations.

Do I have to specify a row height or column width for each frame?

After you define the first frame size, you can use an asterisk (*) to assign the remaining window space to other frames. The asterisk specifies the size as a variable. For example:

```
<FRAMESET ROWS="65,*,60">
```

In this frameset, the middle frame is sized to fit the remaining space left after the other two absolute frames.

Customize Frame Borders

You can change the thickness of your frame borders using the BORDER attribute. By default, Web browsers display the borders around your frames at a thickness of 6 pixels. You can set your frame borders to another size as well as control the color of the borders.

Customize Frame Borders

CHANGE THE FRAME BORDERS

1. Within the `<FRAMESET>` tag, type **BORDER="?"**, replacing *?* with a thickness value, measured in pixels.

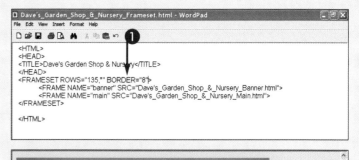

- The Web browser displays the frames with the designated border thickness.

CHANGE THE BORDER COLOR

1. Within the <FRAMESET> tag, type **BORDERCOLOR="?"**, replacing *?* with a color value.

● The Web browser displays the frames with the designated color.

Is there a way to hide my frame borders completely?
Yes. To hide all the frame borders, type **FRAMEBORDER="0"** in the <FRAMESET> tag. This coding makes the content of each separate frame blend together to seemingly make one large Web page. You may experience a small space between the pages. To rid the frame of this space, simply type **BORDER="0"** in the <FRAMESET> tag.

Is there another way I can control frame border thickness?
Yes. You can also use the FRAMESPACING attribute to control the thickness of frame borders. However, only Internet Explorer supports the FRAMESPACING attribute; the attribute is not part of the formal HTML standard. To set a border thickness, type **FRAMESPACING="?"** in the <FRAMESET> tag, replacing *?* with the thickness value you want to set. Border thickness is measured in pixels.

Control Frame Margins

You can control the amount of space that appears between a frame border and the contents of the frame. Using the MARGINWIDTH and MARGINHEIGHT attributes, you can set margins for the top, bottom, left, and right side of your frames. Margin space is measured in pixels.

Control Frame Margins

1. Within the <FRAME> tag, type **MARGINWIDTH="?"**, replacing *?* with the amount of space you want to set for the left and right margins.

2. Type a space and **MARGINHEIGHT="?"**, replacing *?* with the amount of space you want to set for the top and bottom margins.

   The Web browser displays the frames with the designated margins.

   ● In this example, the second frame now has increased margins all around the inside of the frame.

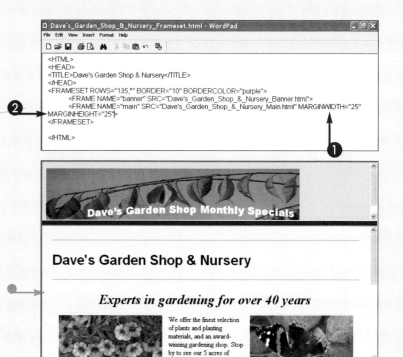

Prevent Frame Resizing

By default, users can resize the frames in your Web page, allowing them to view more information in a frame. You can control your page layout by restricting frame resizing.

Prevent Frame Resizing

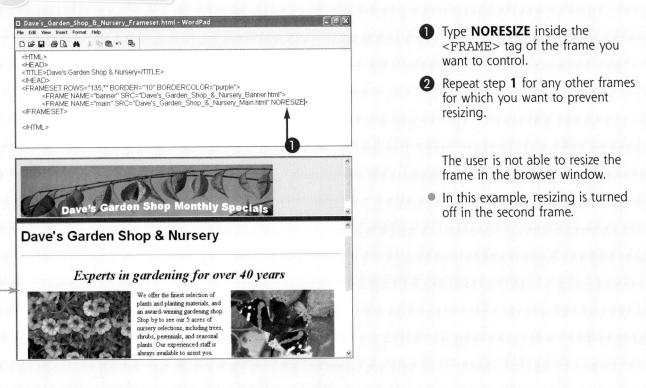

1 Type **NORESIZE** inside the <FRAME> tag of the frame you want to control.

2 Repeat step **1** for any other frames for which you want to prevent resizing.

The user is not able to resize the frame in the browser window.

● In this example, resizing is turned off in the second frame.

Target a Link

To learn how to assign names to frames, see the section "Create Frames."

You can make other pages from your Web site appear in a frame in addition to the initial frameset content. To target links to particular frames, you must identify each frame with a unique name.

Target a Link

1 Open the Web page where the link should appear.

2 Click where you want to insert the link and type **<A HREF="?",** replacing *?* with the target page.

Note: *Be sure to name the frame before targeting a link. See the section "Create Frames" to learn how to name frames in the frameset document.*

```
<HTML>
<HEAD>
<TITLE>Dave's Garden Shop & Nursery</TITLE>
</HEAD>
<BODY BGCOLOR="#A4D4B0">

<H3>Our Top-Selling Perennials: </H3>
<BR>

<TABLE BORDER="2" CELLPADDING="5" CELLSPACING="5">
<TR>
<TD><A HREF="daylily.html"></TD>
</TR>
<TR>
<TD>Poppy</TD>
</TR>
<TR>
<TD>Monkshood</TD>
</TR>
<TR>
<TD>Coreopsis</TD>
</TR>
<TR>
<TD>Bee Balm</TD>
</TR>
</TABLE>
```

3 Type a space and **TARGET="?">,** replacing *?* with the frame name you assigned in step **1**.

```
<HTML>
<HEAD>
<TITLE>Dave's Garden Shop & Nursery</TITLE>
</HEAD>
<BODY BGCOLOR="#A4D4B0">

<H3>Our Top-Selling Perennials: </H3>
<BR>

<TABLE BORDER="2" CELLPADDING="5" CELLSPACING="5">
<TR>
<TD><A HREF="daylily.html" TARGET="main"></TD>
</TR>
<TR>
<TD>Poppy</TD>
</TR>
<TR>
<TD>Monkshood</TD>
</TR>
<TR>
<TD>Coreopsis</TD>
</TR>
<TR>
<TD>Bee Balm</TD>
</TR>
</TABLE>
```

```
<HTML>
<HEAD>
<TITLE>Dave's Garden Shop & Nursery</TITLE>
</HEAD>
<BODY BGCOLOR="#A4D4B0">

<H3>Our Top-Selling Perennials:</H3>
<BR>

<TABLE BORDER="2" CELLPADDING="5" CELLSPACING="5">
<TR>
<TD><A HREF="daylily.html" TARGET="main">Daylily</A></TD>
</TR>
<TR>
<TD>Poppy</TD>
</TR>
<TR>
<TD>Monkshood</TD>
</TR>
<TR>
<TD>Coreopsis</TD>
</TR>
<TR>
<TD>Bee Balm</TD>
</TR>
</TABLE>
```

⑤

④

④ Type the link text.

⑤ Type **</A>**.

You can repeat steps **1** to **5** to target more links.

Dave's Garden Shop Monthly Specials

Our Top-Selling Perennials:

The Daylily is one of our top-selling perennials. It comes in a variety of colors and blooms during the summer. Some varieties bloom throughout the summer season.

Daylily
Poppy
Monkshood
Coreopsis
Bee Balm

● The browser displays the link.

● When the user clicks the link, the page opens in the frame you specified.

Can I make all the links open in the same frame?

Yes. To make all the Web page links open in the same frame, you can add the target frame to the <HEAD> and </HEAD> tags. Simply click within the <HEAD> tags and type **<BASE TARGET="?">**, replacing *?* with the name of the target frame. You must name the target frame in the frameset document in order to reference the name in the <BASE TARGET> tag.

Can I make the target link open a new window?

Yes. You can use the TARGET attribute to instruct the browser to open the target link in a new window. To open the linked page in a new unnamed window, use the _blank value. To open the linked page in the current window, use the _top value. For example:

```
<A HREF="mypage.html"
TARGET="_blank">Click here
to view the page</A>
```

In this code, when the user clicks the link, the document mypage.html opens in a new browser window.

Chapter 11

Creating Forms

Looking for a way to allow your Web site visitors to communicate with you? This chapter shows you how to build forms to gather information from users, and teaches you about the various ways to process the information.

Understanding Forms

You can use forms to collect information from the people who visit your Web site. For example, you might gather answers or feedback from your Web visitors, or enable them to purchase goods or services from your Web site. Before you jump into building your own forms, take a moment to study how forms work and the various ways you can use them on your own Web site.

How Forms Work

Forms use input elements to collect data from a user, such as text fields and check boxes. Once the user fills in the data, he or she can submit the form. As the Web developer, it is up to you to decide how to handle the data. You can write a script to manage form data, receive the data via e-mail, or send the data to a database. Most form data is processed by CGI scripts on the Web server. You can learn more about various ways to process your data in the section "Gather Form Data" later in this chapter.

HTML for Forms

Forms are comprised of three important parts: the <FORM> tag, the form elements, and the submit button. When designing and building a form, you can write HTML to define the form structure and appearance as well as define the different input objects you want to include on the form, such as text fields or radio buttons. All forms should include a Submit button to send the data for processing. You can place your forms directly on a Web page or save them as a separate HTML document and link to the form.

Form Design

Before typing up a form, spend time thinking about how you want the user to interact with the form, what sort of data you want to collect, and how you want the form to appear. Be sure to add label text to your form elements that explains what type of information you want from the user, and give users enough space to enter their input.

Types of Forms

There are several different types of forms you can create. For example, you can add a search form to allow your users to search through your Web site for key information. You can add data collection forms to gather information from users, such as name and e-mail addresses. Your form may be as simple as a guest book or as complex as a detailed survey. You can use forms to customize a user's content, such as displaying the user's name when he or she logs onto your site. You can also use forms to help customers make a purchase on your site.

Controlling Data Entry

You can control how a user enters data into your form input elements. For example, you can guide the user from one input field to the next by controlling the tab order. You can also control the types of data entered into a field. For example, if your form collects phone numbers, you can limit the phone number text element to just inputting numbers instead of characters. You can use JavaScripts to help alert users to invalid form data. See Chapter 13 to learn more about JavaScripts.

Confirmation

After the form data is processed, the script usually displays a message in the browser window noting whether the form data was sent successfully or not. You might also write your own script to send a confirmation message by e-mail. It is always good practice when collecting form data to provide visitors with a confirmation or assurance that some sort of action will be taken based on their contribution.

Types of Form Elements

Forms are comprised of a variety of elements. As you think about how users enter data into a form, you can ascertain the types of elements you might need to include on your own forms.

Text Boxes

Text boxes are input fields designed specifically for users to type data into, such as typing a name or comment. Text boxes can be small to collect limited characters, such as phone numbers, or very large to collect paragraphs of input from the user. You might use text boxes to gather information such as names, addresses, e-mail addresses, feedback comments, and more.

Check Boxes

Check boxes enable a user to make a choice out of a group of choices by activating a value. For example, if you want to collect information on whether the Web site visitor is male or female, you can add two check box options to your form. The user clicks a box to indicate their answer. You can allow users to select just one box or multiple check boxes. For example, you might offer the user check box options regarding their musical preferences, allowing them to select several different styles.

Radio Buttons

Radio buttons are the tiny circle buttons found on forms, named for their resemblance to the buttons found on automobile radios in decades past. You use radio buttons in a group of options. Unlike check boxes, however, the user is allowed to choose only one button to make their choice. For example, if you include a feedback form on your page that rates your Web site, you might present radio buttons for the values Excellent, Good, Average, and Poor. The user can choose only one of the four options.

Menus

Menus are a great way to present a list of choices to a Web page visitor. You can present menus as drop-down lists to free up space on your form. Like radio buttons, users can choose only one item from the menu list. A drop-down list of states, for example, is a common menu found on collection forms. The user scrolls through the list and selects his or her state from the menu.

Submit and Reset Buttons

Every form needs a button the user can press to submit their data. Known as the submit button, this button sends the data to the Web server for processing. Until the user clicks this button, the data is not collected. You might also consider adding a reset button to your page that allows the user to clear all the input fields and start over.

Gather Form Data

After the user enters data into the form, you must determine how to handle the information. Before you begin creating your form, you need to know how the collected data will be processed. Take time to examine your options and set up any necessary procedures with your Web host or on your server.

CGI Scripts

CGI scripts process most data that you collect with forms. CGI, short for Common Gateway Interface, is a script written in a language such as Perl or Java that runs on a Web server. CGI scripts take form data submitted by the user and makes it useful, such as putting it into a database, writing it to a file, creating customized HTML, or sending the information to an e-mail address.

Finding CGI Scripts

You can write your own CGI scripts if you know an appropriate programming language, such as Perl or AppleScript, or you can adapt one of the hundreds of free CGI scripts available on the Web. Sites like The CGI Resource Index (http://cgi.resourceindex.com/), Matt's Script Archive (www.scriptarchive.com/), and ScriptSearch (www.scriptsearch.com) are good places to start. You should also check with your Web host to see what it provides.

CGI and Web Servers

Many Web servers offer CGI scripts for processing form data, but you need to check with your Web host to find out if they feature such processing. If they do, you need to find out the location of the server's CGI-bin. A CGI-bin is a type of directory found on Web servers and may be called something else on different servers. Not all Web hosts allow CGI scripts. If yours does not, you might consider using a form hosting service instead, to process your form results. You can search the Web for form hosting services. Sites such as Creative Digital Resources (www.creative-dr.com) and Response-O-Matic (www.response-o-matic.com) offer free form processing.

Preparing a Script

To make a CGI script ready for your own form, you need to make adjustments to the script variables and path names to suit your Web server. You must also transfer the CGI script to your server, using FTP (File Transfer Protocol). Be sure to check with the Web host regarding where to store the CGI file. Some prefer to store scripts in a central CGI-bin directory, while others let you store scripts in your own folders as long as they utilize a particular file extension.

Sending Data to Databases

Another use for CGI scripts is to send form data to a database. Database programs are designed to store and manage large amounts of data. Client-server databases run 24/7 to process requests from Web users. CGI scripts translate requests from the Web server to a format read by a database, whether the database is located on the same server or in another location. If you plan to use your form data in conjunction with a database, you need to learn more about how databases work with the Web. There are quite a few good books on the subject, including *Web Database Publishing For Dummies* or *Intranet and Web Databases For Dummies*, both from Wiley Publishing, Inc.

Sending Data to an E-mail Address

If you do not want to use a CGI script, you can use an action method to send form data to an e-mail address. This action returns a list of field names and the values entered in each. This option is useful only if the form is simple in nature. More complex forms require scripts or databases to process and make sense of the information. To learn more about sending form data via e-mail, see the section "Send Form Data to an E-mail Address."

Create a Form

You can use a form to gather information from the people who visit your Web site. To create a form, you use the <FORM> tags to define the CGI scripts that will process the form, define the form elements, and define a Submit button to send the data to the CGI script.

Most forms use a CGI script to instruct the Web server to process the collected information. Consult your Web host to find out the location of a CGI script or CGI-bin on the server. You can also forego a CGI script and send the form data to an e-mail address. See the section "Send Form Data to an E-mail Address" to learn more.

Create a Form

① Click where you want to insert a form and type **<FORM METHOD="post"**.

② Type a space and **ACTION="?">**, replacing *?* with the name and location of the CGI script you want to use to process the form data.

Note: You may need to contact your Web host to determine the name and path of the CGI script.

③ Type **</FORM>**.

You can now add input elements to your form.

Note: See the remaining sections in this chapter to learn more about building your form.

Send Form Data to an E-mail Address

You can instruct the browser to send form data to an e-mail address. You might pursue this route if you are creating a simple form or if your Web server does not support CGI scripts.

Send Form Data to an E-Mail Address

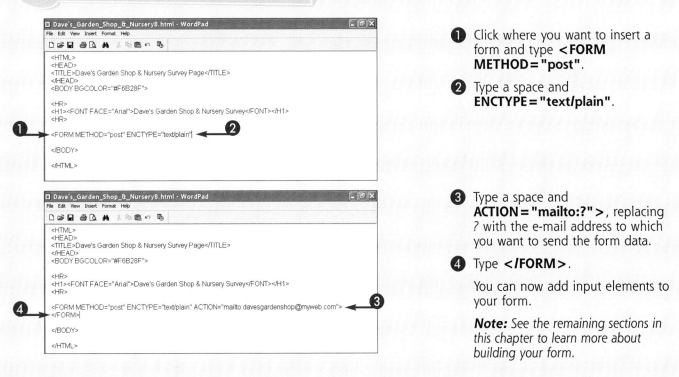

① Click where you want to insert a form and type **<FORM METHOD="post"**.

② Type a space and **ENCTYPE="text/plain"**.

③ Type a space and **ACTION="mailto:?">**, replacing ? with the e-mail address to which you want to send the form data.

④ Type **</FORM>**.

You can now add input elements to your form.

Note: *See the remaining sections in this chapter to learn more about building your form.*

Add a Text Box

By default, browsers display the text box field at a width of 20 characters. You can set a wider text box using the **SIZE** attribute. You can control the number of characters allowed in a text box by specifying a value with the **MAXLENGTH** attribute.

You can add a text box to your form to allow users to type in a single line reply or response. When creating a text box, you must identify the input field with a unique name. You can also control the size and number of characters a user enters into the field.

Add a Text Box

① Between the <FORM> and </FORM> tags add a new line for the text box.

② Type **< INPUT TYPE = "text"**.

③ Type a space and **NAME="?"**, replacing ? with a unique identifier for the text box.

```
<HTML>
<HEAD>
<TITLE>Dave's Garden Shop & Nursery Survey Page</TITLE>
</HEAD>
<BODY BGCOLOR="#F6B28F">

<HR>
<H1><FONT FACE="Arial"><FONT COLOR="004E4A">Dave's Garden Shop & Nursery Survey</FONT></H1>
<HR>

<FORM METHOD="post" ACTION="cgi-bin/survey.pl">
<H3>Thanks for visiting our site. Please take a moment and fill out our survey. Your input will help us to create a better Web site.</H3>

<BR>Where do you purchase most of your gardening materials and supplies?
<INPUT TYPE="text" NAME="purchase">

</FORM>

</BODY>

</HTML>
```

④ Type a space and **SIZE = "?"**, replacing ? with the width in characters you want to assign to the text box.

```
<HTML>
<HEAD>
<TITLE>Dave's Garden Shop & Nursery Survey Page</TITLE>
</HEAD>
<BODY BGCOLOR="#F6B28F">

<HR>
<H1><FONT FACE="Arial"><FONT COLOR="004E4A">Dave's Garden Shop & Nursery Survey</FONT></H1>
<HR>

<FORM METHOD="post" ACTION="cgi-bin/survey.pl">
<H3>Thanks for visiting our site. Please take a moment and fill out our survey. Your input will help us to create a better Web site.</H3>

<BR>Where do you purchase most of your gardening materials and supplies?
<INPUT TYPE="text" NAME="purchase" SIZE="45"

</FORM>

</BODY>

</HTML>
```

```
<HTML>
<HEAD>
<TITLE>Dave's Garden Shop & Nursery Survey Page</TITLE>
</HEAD>
<BODY BGCOLOR="#F6B28F">

<HR>
<H1><FONT FACE="Arial"><FONT COLOR="004E4A">Dave's Garden Shop & Nursery Survey</FONT></H1>
<HR>

<FORM METHOD="post" ACTION="cgi-bin/survey.pl">
<H3>Thanks for visiting our site. Please take a moment and fill out our survey. Your input will help us to create a
better Web site.</H3>

<BR>Where do you purchase most of your gardening materials and supplies?
<INPUT TYPE="text" NAME="purchase" SIZE="45" MAXLENGTH="40">

</FORM>

</BODY>

</HTML>
```

❺

❺ To define a maximum number of characters for the field, type **MAXLENGTH="?">** , replacing *?* with the maximum number of characters allowed.

Note: *Do not forget to type a closing bracket (>) at the end of your input element tag.*

Dave's Garden Shop & Nursery Survey

Thanks for visiting our site. Please take a moment and fill out our survey. Your input will help us to create a better Web site.

Where do you purchase most of your gardening materials and supplies?

Local garden center

● The Web browser displays the text box in the form.

● The user can click inside the text box and type the required information.

Can I add a default value to a text box?
Yes. A default value is text that already appears in the text box when the user views the form. You can use default values to display instructions about the type of data required, give users an example of what data you are looking for, or specify a popular choice or response. To specify a default, you can add the VALUE attribute to the <INPUT> tag. For example:

```
<FORM METHOD="post"
ACTION="/cgi-
bin/feedback.pl">

<INPUT TYPE="text"
NAME="email" VALUE="Enter your
e-mail address">

</FORM>
```

How do I create a password text box?
Browsers handle password text boxes a bit differently than regular text boxes. Instead of seeing what is typed in the input field, the data appears as asterisks (*) instead of characters. This prevents others from seeing the password text. To create a text box for password entry, you specify the password type in the <INPUT> tag. Your code might look like this:

```
<FORM METHOD="post"
ACTION="/cgi-
bin/feedback.pl">

<INPUT TYPE="password"
NAME="password" SIZE="45">
</FORM>
```

Add a Large Text Area

If your form requires a larger text entry box, you can create a large text area for multiple lines of text. For example, if you create a feedback form, you can use a large text area to allow users to type in paragraphs of text.

When defining a text area, you can control the size of the text box and how text wraps within the field. Text area size is measured in rows and columns, based on character height.

Add a Large Text Area

1 Between the <FORM> and </FORM> tags add a new line for the large text box.

2 Type **<TEXTAREA**.

3 Type a space and **NAME="?"**, replacing *?* with a unique name for the text area.

   Note: *You can use the <BR> or <P> tags to separate input elements onto new lines in your form.*

```
<HTML>
<HEAD>
<TITLE>Dave's Garden Shop & Nursery Survey Page</TITLE>
</HEAD>
<BODY BGCOLOR="#F6B28F">

<HR>
<H1><FONT FACE="Arial"><FONT COLOR="004E4A">Dave's Garden Shop & Nursery Survey</FONT></H1>
<HR>

<FORM METHOD="post" ACTION="cgi-bin/survey.pl">
<H3>Thanks for visiting our site. Please take a moment and fill out our survey. Your input will help us to create a
better Web site.</H3>

<BR>What gardening information would you like to see on our site?
<TEXTAREA NAME="gardeninfo"

<BR>Where do you purchase most of your gardening materials and supplies?
<INPUT TYPE="text" NAME="purchase" SIZE="45" MAXLENGTH="40">

</FORM>

</BODY>

</HTML>
```

4 Type a space and **ROWS="?"**, replacing *?* with the number of rows you want to specify to determine the height of the text area.

5 Type a space and type **COLS="?"**, replacing *?* with the number of character columns you want to specify to determine the width of the text area.

```
<HTML>
<HEAD>
<TITLE>Dave's Garden Shop & Nursery Survey Page</TITLE>
</HEAD>
<BODY BGCOLOR="#F6B28F">

<HR>
<H1><FONT FACE="Arial"><FONT COLOR="004E4A">Dave's Garden Shop & Nursery Survey</FONT></H1>
<HR>

<FORM METHOD="post" ACTION="cgi-bin/survey.pl">
<H3>Thanks for visiting our site. Please take a moment and fill out our survey. Your input will help us to create a
better Web site.</H3>

<BR>What gardening information would you like to see on our site?
<TEXTAREA NAME="gardeninfo" ROWS="10" COLS="70"

<BR>Where do you purchase most of your gardening materials and supplies?
<INPUT TYPE="text" NAME="purchase" SIZE="45" MAXLENGTH="40">

</FORM>

</BODY>

</HTML>
```

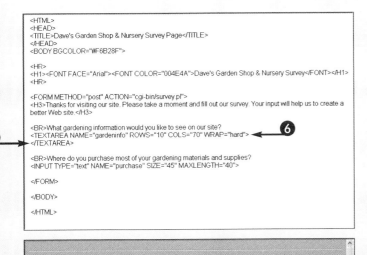

```
<HTML>
<HEAD>
<TITLE>Dave's Garden Shop & Nursery Survey Page</TITLE>
</HEAD>
<BODY BGCOLOR="#F6B28F">

<HR>
<H1><FONT FACE="Arial"><FONT COLOR="004E4A">Dave's Garden Shop & Nursery Survey</FONT></H1>
<HR>

<FORM METHOD="post" ACTION="cgi-bin/survey.pl">
<H3>Thanks for visiting our site. Please take a moment and fill out our survey. Your input will help us to create a
better Web site.</H3>

<BR>What gardening information would you like to see on our site?
<TEXTAREA NAME="gardeninfo" ROWS="10" COLS="70" WRAP="hard">
</TEXTAREA>

<BR>Where do you purchase most of your gardening materials and supplies?
<INPUT TYPE="text" NAME="purchase" SIZE="45" MAXLENGTH="40">

</FORM>

</BODY>

</HTML>
```

Dave's Garden Shop & Nursery Survey

Thanks for visiting our site. Please take a moment and fill out our survey. Your input
will help us to create a better Web site.

What gardening information would you like to see on our site?
Information about when to plant shrubs and trees

Where do you purchase most of your gardening materials and supplies?

6 Type a space and **WRAP="?">**, replacing
? with a text wrap control:

soft wraps text within the text area, but will
not wrap text in the form results.

hard wraps text both within the text area
and the form results.

off turns off text wrapping, forcing the user
to create new lines of text as they type.

7 Type **</TEXTAREA>**.

● The Web browser displays the text box in
the form.

● The user can click inside the text box and
type information.

**What happens if the user types more
than can be viewed in the text area?**
If the user types more
text than what is visible
in the text area, scroll
bars appear active at
the side of the text
box. Scroll bars
allow the user to
scroll and view the
text. The text area
automatically
holds as much text
as the user needs to
type, up to 32,700
characters.

**Is there a way to keep users from
entering text into a large text area?**
Yes. You can use the
READONLY attribute
if you want to type
default text into a
text area and do
not want users to
move or edit the
text. For example,
you might use a
large text area to
explain something about
your form or offer detailed instructions. You
can place the READONLY attribute within
the <TEXTAREA> and </TEXTAREA>
tags.

Add Check Boxes

You can add check boxes to your form to allow users to select from one or more options. You can group the check boxes under a single **NAME** attribute.

```
<FORM>
<INPUT TYPE="checkbox"
NAME="favoritecolors"
VALUE="blue">
</FORM>
```

www.mywebpage

① Between the <FORM> and </FORM> tags type **<INPUT TYPE="checkbox"**.

② Type a space and **NAME="?"**, replacing ? with a unique name for the check box or check box group.

```
<HTML>
<HEAD>
<TITLE>Dave's Garden Shop & Nursery Survey Page</TITLE>
</HEAD>
<BODY BGCOLOR="#F6B28F">

<HR>
<H1><FONT FACE="Arial"><FONT COLOR="004E4A">Dave's Garden Shop & Nursery Survey</FONT>
</H1>
<HR>

<FORM METHOD="post" ACTION="cgi-bin/survey.pl">
<H3>Thanks for visiting our site. Please take a moment and fill out our survey. Your input will help us to create a better Web site.</H3>

<BR>How did you learn about our site?

<BR>Did you find the information you were looking for?
<BR><INPUT TYPE="checkbox" NAME="find">

<BR>What gardening information would you like to see on our site?
<TEXTAREA NAME="gardeninfo" ROWS="10" COLS="70" WRAP="hard">
</TEXTAREA>

<BR>Where do you purchase most of your gardening materials and supplies?
<INPUT TYPE="text" NAME="purchase" SIZE="45" MAXLENGTH="40">

</FORM>
```

③ Type a space and **VALUE="?">**, replacing ? with a value describing the check box.

Note: The check box value does not appear on the form.

```
<HTML>
<HEAD>
<TITLE>Dave's Garden Shop & Nursery Survey Page</TITLE>
</HEAD>
<BODY BGCOLOR="#F6B28F">

<HR>
<H1><FONT FACE="Arial"><FONT COLOR="004E4A">Dave's Garden Shop & Nursery Survey</FONT>
</H1>
<HR>

<FORM METHOD="post" ACTION="cgi-bin/survey.pl">
<H3>Thanks for visiting our site. Please take a moment and fill out our survey. Your input will help us to create a better Web site.</H3>

<BR>How did you learn about our site?

<BR>Did you find the information you were looking for?
<BR><INPUT TYPE="checkbox" NAME="find" VALUE="yesanswer">

<BR>What gardening information would you like to see on our site?
<TEXTAREA NAME="gardeninfo" ROWS="10" COLS="70" WRAP="hard">
</TEXTAREA>

<BR>Where do you purchase most of your gardening materials and supplies?
<INPUT TYPE="text" NAME="purchase" SIZE="45" MAXLENGTH="40">

</FORM>
```

```
<HTML>
<HEAD>
<TITLE>Dave's Garden Shop & Nursery Survey Page</TITLE>
</HEAD>
<BODY BGCOLOR="#F6B28F">

<HR>
<H1><FONT FACE="Arial"><FONT COLOR="004E4A">Dave's Garden Shop & Nursery Survey</FONT>
</H1>
<HR>

<FORM METHOD="post" ACTION="cgi-bin/survey.pl">
<H3>Thanks for visiting our site. Please take a moment and fill out our survey. Your input will help us to create a
better Web site.</H3>

<BR>How did you learn about our site?

<BR>Did you find the information you were looking for?
<BR><INPUT TYPE="checkbox" NAME="find" VALUE="yesanswer">Yes          4
<BR><INPUT TYPE="checkbox" NAME="find" VALUE="noanswer">No

<BR>What gardening information would you like to see on our site?
<TEXTAREA NAME="gardeninfo" ROWS="10" COLS="70" WRAP="hard">
</TEXTAREA>

<BR>Where do you purchase most of your gardening materials and supplies?
<INPUT TYPE="text" NAME="purchase" SIZE="45" MAXLENGTH="40">
```

⑤

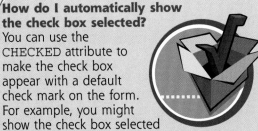

Dave's Garden Shop & Nursery Survey

Thanks for visiting our site. Please take a moment and fill out our survey. Your input will help us to create a better Web site.

How did you learn about our site?

Did you find the information you were looking for?
☑Yes
☐No

What gardening information would you like to see on our site?

④ Type the text you want to appear beside the check box.

⑤ Repeat steps **1** to **5** to create more check boxes for a group of check box options.

Note: *You can use the <BR> or <P> tags to separate input elements onto new lines in your form.*

● The Web browser displays the check box in the form.

● The user can click the box to insert a check mark.

How do I automatically show the check box selected?

You can use the CHECKED attribute to make the check box appear with a default check mark on the form. For example, you might show the check box selected if the option is a popular choice or expect most users to select the option. You can add the CHECKED attribute to the <INPUT> tag, as in this example:

<FORM METHOD="post" ACTION="/ cgi-bin/questionnaire.pl">

<INPUT TYPE="checkbox" NAME= "favoritecolors" VALUE="Blue" CHECKED>

</FORM>

My check boxes appear on one line. How do I separate them onto separate lines in the form?

You can use the <P> or <BR> tags to make each check box appear on a separate line. Your code might look like this:

<FORM METHOD="post" ACTION="/cgi-bin/ questionnaire.pl">

<P>What type of movie do you like the best?</P>

<INPUT TYPE="checkbox" NAME="genre" VALUE="Drama">

<INPUT TYPE="checkbox" NAME="genre" VALUE="Comedy">

<INPUT TYPE="checkbox" NAME="genre" VALUE="Action">

<INPUT TYPE="checkbox" NAME="genre" VALUE="Horror">

</FORM>

Add Radio Buttons

You can use radio buttons if you want to present a choice of items on a form, yet allow the user to choose only one item from the group. The user clicks a button to activate the selection.

```
<FORM>
INPUT TYPE="radio"
NAME="pet"
VALUE="cat"
</FORM>
```

www.mywebpage

Add Radio Buttons

1 Between the `<FORM>` and `</FORM>` tags type **`<INPUT TYPE="radio"`**.

2 Type a space and **`NAME="?"`**, replacing *?* with a unique name for the radio button group.

```
</H1>
<HR>

<FORM METHOD="post" ACTION="cgi-bin/survey.pl">
<H3>Thanks for visiting our site. Please take a moment and fill out our survey. Your input will help us to create a
better Web site.</H3>

<BR>How did you learn about our site?
<BR><INPUT TYPE="radio" NAME="learn"                    ← 2

<BR>Did you find the information you were looking for?
<BR><INPUT TYPE="checkbox" NAME="find" VALUE="yesanswer">Yes
<BR><INPUT TYPE="checkbox" NAME="find" VALUE="noanswer">No

<BR>
<BR>What gardening information would you like to see on our site?
<TEXTAREA NAME="gardeninfo" ROWS="10" COLS="70" WRAP="hard">
</TEXTAREA>

<BR>Where do you purchase most of your gardening materials and supplies?
<INPUT TYPE="text" NAME="purchase" SIZE="45" MAXLENGTH="40">

</FORM>

</BODY>

</HTML>
```

3 Type a space and **`VALUE="?">`**, replacing *?* with a value describing the radio button.

Note: *The radio button value does not appear on the form.*

```
</H1>
<HR>

<FORM METHOD="post" ACTION="cgi-bin/survey.pl">
<H3>Thanks for visiting our site. Please take a moment and fill out our survey. Your input will help us to create a
better Web site.</H3>

<BR>How did you learn about our site?
<BR><INPUT TYPE="radio" NAME="learn" VALUE="search">     ← 3

<BR>Did you find the information you were looking for?
<BR><INPUT TYPE="checkbox" NAME="find" VALUE="yesanswer">Yes
<BR><INPUT TYPE="checkbox" NAME="find" VALUE="noanswer">No

<BR>
<BR>What gardening information would you like to see on our site?
<TEXTAREA NAME="gardeninfo" ROWS="10" COLS="70" WRAP="hard">
</TEXTAREA>

<BR>Where do you purchase most of your gardening materials and supplies?
<INPUT TYPE="text" NAME="purchase" SIZE="45" MAXLENGTH="40">

</FORM>

</BODY>

</HTML>
```

```
<HR>
<H1><FONT FACE="Arial"><FONT COLOR="004E4A">Dave's Garden Shop & Nursery Survey</FONT>
</H1>
<HR>

<FORM METHOD="post" ACTION="cgi-bin/survey.pl">
<H3>Thanks for visiting our site. Please take a moment and fill out our survey. Your input will help us to create a
better Web site.</H3>

<BR>How did you learn about our site?
<BR><INPUT TYPE="radio" NAME="learn" VALUE="search">Random search          ←  4
<BR><INPUT TYPE="radio" NAME="learn" VALUE="advert">Advertisement
<BR><INPUT TYPE="radio" NAME="learn" VALUE="friend">Friend or family member
<BR><INPUT TYPE="radio" NAME="learn" VALUE="other">Other <INPUT TYPE="text" NAME="other"
SIZE="45">|

<BR>Did you find the information you were looking for?
<BR><INPUT TYPE="checkbox" NAME="find" VALUE="yesanswer">Yes
<BR><INPUT TYPE="checkbox" NAME="find" VALUE="noanswer">No

<BR>
<BR>What gardening information would you like to see on our site?
<TEXTAREA NAME="gardeninfo" ROWS="10" COLS="70" WRAP="hard">
</TEXTAREA>

<BR>Where do you purchase most of your gardening materials and supplies?
<INPUT TYPE="text" NAME="purchase" SIZE="45" MAXLENGTH="40">
```

4 Type the text you want to appear beside the radio button.

5 Repeat steps **1** to **5** to add more radio buttons to the group.

Note: You can use the <BR> or <P> tags to separate input elements onto new lines in your form.

Dave's Garden Shop & Nursery Survey

Thanks for visiting our site. Please take a moment and fill out our survey. Your input will help us to create a better Web site.

How did you learn about our site?
- ○ Random search
- ○ Advertisement
- ○ Friend or family member
- ○ Other [_____]

Did you find the information you were looking for?
- ☐ Yes
- ☐ No

What gardening information would you like to see on our site?

- The Web browser displays the radio buttons in the form.

- The user can click the box to insert a check mark.

Should the radio button value be the same text as the NAME attribute?

Not necessarily. You use the NAME attribute to group related items and identify the radio button in the processing script. The VALUE attribute is the text sent to the server if a user selects the button. If you do not set the VALUE attribute, the word "on" is sent to the script, which does not tell you which button the user selected. For simplicity's sake, Web developers usually assign the same name to both the NAME attribute and the VALUE attribute.

Can I show a particular radio button selected by default?

Yes. You can use the CHECKED attribute to show one radio button in the group selected by default. You can add the CHECKED attribute after the VALUE attribute in your HTML code. Your code might look like this:

```
<FORM METHOD="post"
ACTION="/cgi-
bin/questionnaire.pl">

<INPUT TYPE="radio"
NAME="agerange"
VALUE="40-50"
CHECKED>

</FORM>
```

Add a
Menu List

You can add a menu to a form to give users a list of choices. Menu lists allow you to display choices as a drop-down list that displays only when the user selects the list. By storing choices in a drop-down list, you can free up space for other input items on the form.

Add a Menu List

① Between the <FORM> and </FORM> tags type **<SELECT NAME="?"**, replacing *?* with a unique name for the menu.

② Type a space and **SIZE="?">**, replacing *?* with the height, measured in character lines, for the menu input.

If you want to display a drop-down menu, set the height to 1.

③ Start a new line and type **<OPTION VALUE="?">**, replacing *?* with a descriptive word for the menu item.

④ Type the text you want to appear in the menu list.

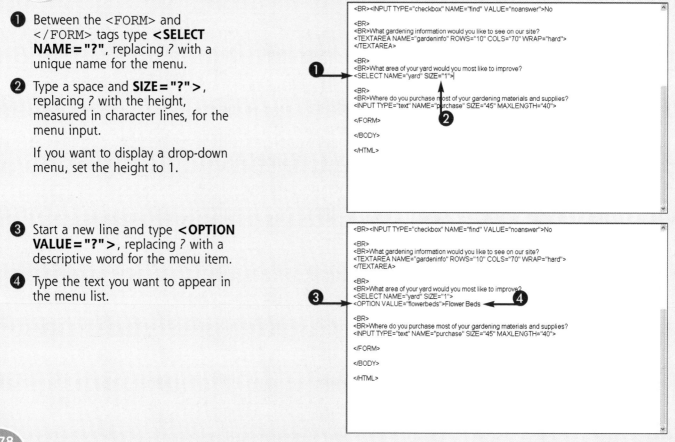

```
<BR><INPUT TYPE="checkbox" NAME="find" VALUE="noanswer">No

<BR>
<BR>What gardening information would you like to see on our site?
<TEXTAREA NAME="gardeninfo" ROWS="10" COLS="70" WRAP="hard">
</TEXTAREA>

<BR>
<BR>What area of your yard would you most like to improve?
<SELECT NAME="yard" SIZE="1">

<BR>
<BR>Where do you purchase most of your gardening materials and supplies?
<INPUT TYPE="text" NAME="purchase" SIZE="45" MAXLENGTH="40">

</FORM>

</BODY>

</HTML>
```

```
<BR><INPUT TYPE="checkbox" NAME="find" VALUE="noanswer">No

<BR>
<BR>What gardening information would you like to see on our site?
<TEXTAREA NAME="gardeninfo" ROWS="10" COLS="70" WRAP="hard">
</TEXTAREA>

<BR>
<BR>What area of your yard would you most like to improve?
<SELECT NAME="yard" SIZE="1">
<OPTION VALUE="flowerbeds">Flower Beds

<BR>
<BR>Where do you purchase most of your gardening materials and supplies?
<INPUT TYPE="text" NAME="purchase" SIZE="45" MAXLENGTH="40">

</FORM>

</BODY>

</HTML>
```

```
<BR><INPUT TYPE="checkbox" NAME="find" VALUE="noanswer">No

<BR>
<BR>What gardening information would you like to see on our site?
<TEXTAREA NAME="gardeninfo" ROWS="10" COLS="70" WRAP="hard">
</TEXTAREA>

<BR>
<BR>What area of your yard would you most like to improve?
<SELECT NAME="yard" SIZE="1">
<OPTION VALUE="flowerbeds">Flower Beds
<OPTION VALUE="deck">Deck Area
<OPTION VALUE="grass">Grassy Areas
<OPTION VALUE="frontyard" SELECTED>Front Yard
<OPTION VALUE="backyard">Back Yard
<OPTION VALUE="sideyard">Side Yard
</SELECT>

<BR>
<BR>Where do you purchase most of your gardening materials and supplies?
<INPUT TYPE="text" NAME="purchase" SIZE="45" MAXLENGTH="40">

</FORM>

</BODY>

</HTML>
```

5

7

6

○ Advertisement
○ Friend or family member
○ Other

Did you find the information you were looking for?
☐ Yes
☐ No

What gardening information would you like to see on our site?

What area of your yard would you most like to improve? | Front Yard ▾ |

Flower Beds
Deck Area
Grassy Areas
Front Yard
Back Yard

Where do you purchase most of your gardening materia

5 Repeat steps **3** and **4** to add more menu items to the list.

6 To make one menu item appear selected in the list, type **SELECTED** after the VALUE attribute.

7 Type **</SELECT>**.

The Web browser displays the menu on the form.

● The user can click to display the drop-down list and click to make a selection.

How do I display the entire menu in my form?

Simply enter the number of menu entries as the SIZE attribute value. This makes the menu appear at a height that shows all the items in the list. If the menu list is long, you may end up taking up more room than you like on the form, making users scroll to view the selections. If you prefer to save room on your form, keep the menu size at 1. This creates a drop-down menu list.

Can I create a submenu?

Yes. You can group your menu items into categories to create submenus using the <OPTGROUP> tag. You can use the LABEL attribute to add a title to each submenu. Your HTML code might look like this:

```
<P>What is favorite flower?</P>
<SELECT NAME="favoriteflower">
<OPTGROUP LABEL="Perennial">
<OPTION VALUE="Daisy">Daisy
<OPTION VALUE="Lily">Lily
<OPTION VALUE="Rose">Rose
</OPTGROUP>
<OPGROUP LABEL="Annual">
<OPTION VALUE="Petunia">Petunia
<OPTION VALUE="Impatiens">Impatiens
<OPTION VALUE="Pansy">Pansy
</OPTGROUP>
</SELECT>
```

Not all browsers support the <OPTGROUP> tag.

Add a Submit Button

Add a submit button to your form so users can send you the data they enter. Most Web page developers add the submit button to the bottom of the form. You can choose any label you like for the button, as long as it is easy for users to understand that they need to click it to submit their data.

Add a Submit Button

1 Between the <FORM> and </FORM> tags type **<INPUT TYPE="submit"**.

2 Type a space and type **VALUE="?">**, replacing *?* with the text you want to appear on the button.

```
<TEXTAREA NAME="gardeninfo" ROWS="10" COLS="70" WRAP="hard">
</TEXTAREA>

<BR>
<BR>What area of your yard would you most like to improve?
<SELECT NAME="yard" SIZE="1">
<OPTION VALUE="flowerbeds">Flower Beds
<OPTION VALUE="deck">Deck Area
<OPTION VALUE="grass">Grassy Areas
<OPTION VALUE="frontyard" SELECTED>Front Yard
<OPTION VALUE="backyard">Back Yard
<OPTION VALUE="sideyard">Side Yard
<OPTION VALUE="shade">Add Shade
</SELECT>

<BR>
<BR>Where do you purchase most of your gardening materials and supplies?
<INPUT TYPE="text" NAME="purchase" SIZE="45" MAXLENGTH="40">

<BR>
<BR><INPUT TYPE="submit" VALUE="Submit">|     ← 2

</FORM>

</BODY>

</HTML>
                                              1
```

● The browser displays the button on the form.

When the user clicks the button, the form data is processed as specified in the <FORM> tag.

```
○ Other
Did you find the information you were looking for?
☐ Yes
☐ No
What gardening information would you like to see on our site?



What area of your yard would you most like to improve?  Front Yard ▾
Where do you purchase most of your gardening materials and supplies?

Submit
```

Add a Reset Button

You can add a reset button to your form to allow users to clear the data. For example, the user may want to enter a different set of information, or change his or her mind about submitting the information. A reset button lets users erase all the information they entered into the various input fields.

Add a Reset Button

```
<TEXTAREA NAME="gardeninfo" ROWS="10" COLS="70" WRAP="hard">
</TEXTAREA>

<BR>
<BR>What area of your yard would you most like to improve?
<SELECT NAME="yard" SIZE="1">
<OPTION VALUE="flowerbeds">Flower Beds
<OPTION VALUE="deck">Deck Area
<OPTION VALUE="grass">Grassy Areas
<OPTION VALUE="frontyard" SELECTED>Front Yard
<OPTION VALUE="backyard">Back Yard
<OPTION VALUE="sideyard">Side Yard
<OPTION VALUE="shade">Add Shade
</SELECT>

<BR>
<BR>Where do you purchase most of your gardening materials and supplies?
<INPUT TYPE="text" NAME="purchase" SIZE="45" MAXLENGTH="40">

<BR>
<BR><INPUT TYPE="submit" VALUE="Submit">  <INPUT TYPE="reset" VALUE="Reset">|       ②

</FORM>

</BODY>

</HTML>
```

① Between the `<FORM>` and `</FORM>` tags type **<INPUT TYPE = "reset"**.

② Type a space and type **VALUE = "?" >**, replacing *?* with the text you want to appear on the button.

○ Other ▢▢▢▢▢▢▢

Did you find the information you were looking for?
▢ Yes
▢ No

What gardening information would you like to see on our site?

What area of your yard would you most like to improve? Front Yard ▾

Where do you purchase most of your gardening materials and supplies?

[Submit] [Reset] ◄

● The browser displays the button on the form.

When the user clicks the button, the form is reset to its original settings.

Chapter 12

Adding Sounds and Videos

You can make your Web pages more exciting by adding multimedia elements. This chapter shows you how to add sound and video files to your HTML pages.

Understanding Multimedia Elements

The term *multimedia* encompasses all kinds of dynamic visual and audio data on the Internet and computers in general. Graphics, sound, animation, and movies are all examples of multimedia elements. You can incorporate your own multimedia elements onto your HTML pages. Before attempting to add your own multimedia elements, first make sure you understand how such elements work among Web pages, as well as how such elements will affect the person viewing the page.

Ways to Use Multimedia

You can use media files in a variety of ways on your Web page. Media can create an ambiance for the site, enhance your site's message, illustrate a product or service, or simply entertain. When choosing a media file and format to add to your page, always consider the main target audience for your pages. Be sure to include information about the multimedia elements on your page in case the user wants to turn them off or is unable to view or play them.

Delivering Media Files

You can deliver multimedia files to the users viewing your pages in several ways. You can link to an external media file, embed the file into your page, or stream the file. The method you choose depends on the way in which you want the user to interact with the file. Regardless of the method, you must specify the location of the file, and include the file on the server in which you publish your Web page.

External Media Files

One way to incorporate a multimedia element into your page is to supply a link to an external media file. For example, you might allow a visitor to click a link and download a slide show of your vacation pictures, or download a music file of your latest song. If the user decides to access the file, the browser helps him or her determine how to conduct the download and where to store the file. Once the file is downloaded, the user can play the file in a separate window using the appropriate media player or program.

Embedded Files

You can integrate a multimedia file directly onto your page by embedding the file. When the user activates the file, it plays as part of the Web page. For example, you might embed a video file to play in an area on the Web page. Depending on the file type and setup, the file may play immediately when the user displays the page, or when the user activates a button or other feature on the page.

Streaming Media

With streaming media, the user can immediately start viewing or hearing the file as the rest of it continues to download. The data starts downloading into a buffer and then the media player begins playing the file. Adding streaming media to your page is similar to linking or embedding a file, yet instead of referencing the actual file, you define a meta file that contains information about the target file's location.

Understanding Plug-ins and Players

A wide variety of media formats exist on the Internet, but in order to actually play these formats, the end user needs a plug-in or media player. When determining what type of media file you want to include with your page, think about how your target audience will interact with the file. Do they need a special plug-in or player program to play the file? If so, you need to add information on your page about the requirements along with access to the actual media file.

Plug-ins

Plug-ins are specialized applications that work along with the browser to play a media file, typically focusing on a particular file format. If a user does not have a particular plug-in for the type of file you offer, they can easily download it, install it, and use it as part of their Web browser. First introduced by Netscape, plug-ins are now popular among all the browsers.

Media Players

Media players are separate programs designed to handle numerous types of media files. Often called *all-in-one players*, media players can work both separately and alongside browsers to play multimedia files encountered on and off the Web. Popular media players include Microsoft's Windows Media Player, RealNetworks' RealOne Player, and Apple's QuickTime player. Users can download copies of these popular media players from the Internet, or you can provide links to the sites.

Dueling HTML Elements

Establishing standards for Web page development is an ongoing task for the World Wide Web Consortium (W3C). Currently, two popular elements exist for showing multimedia files on Web pages, the EMBED and OBJECT elements. Netscape created the non-standard EMBED element, while the W3C introduced the standard OBJECT element. Microsoft added ActiveX controls to the OBJECT element. Today's browser versions support different degrees of these elements. For the widest support, many developers combine the OBJECT element with the non-standard EMBED element.

Embed with ActiveX Controls

Another way you can embed video clips into your pages is using ActiveX controls along with the <OBJECT> element. ActiveX uses a CLASSID attribute control number to define which data type the browser loads for playback. The CLASSID attribute for QuickTime, for example, is a different number than that for Windows Media Player. Once you define the proper player, you can set the parameters for the clip's playback.

Finding Media Players and Plug-ins

Player	Web Site
Windows Media Player	www.microsoft.com/downloads
QuickTime	www.apple.com/quicktime
RealOne Player	www.real.com
Macromedia Flash Player	www.macromedia.com
Macromedia Shockwave Player	www.macromedia.com
Adobe Acrobat Reader	www.adobe.com/products/acrobat/main.html
Netscape Plug-ins	http://channels.netscape.com/ns/browsers/plugins.jsp

Link to Audio or Video Files

You can insert links on your Web page that, when clicked, download and play an audio or video file. When you link to a file, the file opens to play in a separate window. Linking is the easiest way to deliver multimedia files to your Web page visitor.

When publishing your HTML page to a Web server, make sure you upload the audio or video file along with the document.

Link to Audio or Video Files

 Type the text you want to use as a link.

② Type **<A HREF="?">** in front of the link text, replacing the *?* with the location and name of the audio or video file to which you want to link.

Note: See Chapter 8 to learn more about creating HTML links.

❸ Type **</A>** at the end of the link text.

```
<HR SIZE="3" NOSHADE>
<H1><FONT FACE="Arial">Dave's Garden Shop & Nursery</FONT></H1>
<HR SIZE="3" NOSHADE>

<CENTER><P><FONT SIZE="4"><B><I>Experts in gardening for over 40 years</I></B></FONT></P>
</CENTER>

<IMG SRC="Million_Bells2.jpg" ALIGN="Left" HSPACE="15">
<IMG SRC="Butterfly3.jpg" ALIGN="Right" HSPACE="15">

<P>We offer the finest selection of plants and planting materials, and an award-winning gardening shop. Stop
by to see our 5 acres of nursery selections, including trees, shrubs, annuals, perennials, and seasonal plants.
Our experienced staff is always available to assist you.</P><BR CLEAR="All">
<BR>

<P>Be sure to visit our store for garden-themed gifts for indoors and outdoors. We feature exciting new items
for home decorating and gardening at the start of each season.</P>

<IMG SRC="Garden_Supplies.jpg" WIDTH="300" HEIGHT="200" ALT="Image of Gardening Tool"
ALIGN="middle">   
Click <A HREF="classical1.mp3">here to listen to a selection from our gardening music collection.

</BODY>

</HTML>
```

❷   ❶

```
<HR SIZE="3" NOSHADE>
<H1><FONT FACE="Arial">Dave's Garden Shop & Nursery</FONT></H1>
<HR SIZE="3" NOSHADE>

<CENTER><P><FONT SIZE="4"><B><I>Experts in gardening for over 40 years</I></B></FONT></P>
</CENTER>

<IMG SRC="Million_Bells2.jpg" ALIGN="Left" HSPACE="15">
<IMG SRC="Butterfly3.jpg" ALIGN="Right" HSPACE="15">

<P>We offer the finest selection of plants and planting materials, and an award-winning gardening shop. Stop
by to see our 5 acres of nursery selections, including trees, shrubs, annuals, perennials, and seasonal plants.
Our experienced staff is always available to assist you.</P><BR CLEAR="All">
<BR>

<P>Be sure to visit our store for garden-themed gifts for indoors and outdoors. We feature exciting new items
for home decorating and gardening at the start of each season.</P>

<IMG SRC="Garden_Supplies.jpg" WIDTH="300" HEIGHT="200" ALT="Image of Gardening Tool"
ALIGN="middle">   
Click <A HREF="classical1.mp3">here</A> to listen to a selection from our gardening music collection.

</BODY>

</HTML>
```

❸

an award-winning gardening shop. Stop by to see our 5 acres of nursery selections, including trees, shrubs, annuals, perennials, and seasonal plants. Our experienced staff is always available to assist you.

Be sure to visit our store for garden-themed gifts for indoors and outdoors. We feature exciting new items for home decorating and gardening at the start of each season.

Click here to listen to a selection from our gardening music collection.

The Web browser displays the link on the page.

● When the user activates the link, the Web browser attempts to play the audio or video file.

Note: *See Chapter 2 to learn more about viewing your HTML document as an offline Web page.*

In this example, Windows Media Player opens and plays the audio file.

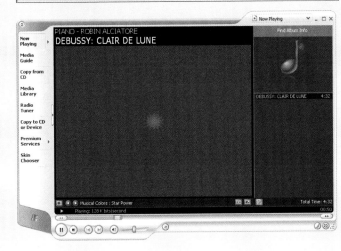

Does my page need to include information about the file available for downloading?

It is always good practice to give your Web page visitors all the information they need to know in order to download and view any type of multimedia file. For example, include a brief description of the file, list the file type and size, and provide a link to any plug-ins or media players the user might need in order to play the file.

What happens if the link is broken?

If users attempt to activate a link to an inactive URL, their Web browser displays an error message. Always check your links as part of your Web page maintenance after the page is published. Be careful not to move any referenced files or you will need to rewrite the link to the correct file.

Embed an Audio File

You can add an embedded sound to your HTML page using the <EMBED> tag. Embedded sounds play directly from your page. Playback controls appear on the page allowing the user to start and stop the sound.

You can control the size of the sound controls that appear with an embedded sound file. For example, you can set the width at 170 pixels and the height at 25 pixels to create easy-to-read playback controls.

Embed an Audio File

① Type **<EMBED SRC="?">** where you want to insert sound controls on the page, replacing the ? with the location and name of the audio file.

```
<HR SIZE="3" NOSHADE>

<CENTER><P><FONT SIZE="4"><B><I>Experts in gardening for over 40 years</I></B></FONT></P>
</CENTER>

<IMG SRC="Million_Bells2.jpg" ALIGN="Left" HSPACE="15">
<IMG SRC="Butterfly3.jpg" ALIGN="Right" HSPACE="15">

<P>We offer the finest selection of plants and planting materials, and an award-winning gardening shop. Stop
by to see our 5 acres of nursery selections, including trees, shrubs, annuals, perennials, and seasonal plants.
Our experienced staff is always available to assist you.</P><BR CLEAR="All">
<BR>

<P>Be sure to visit our store for garden-themed gifts for indoors and outdoors. We feature exciting new items
for home decorating and gardening at the start of each season.</P>

<IMG SRC="Garden_Supplies.jpg" WIDTH="300" HEIGHT="200" ALT="Image of Gardening Tool"
ALIGN="left">   
Music for the Garden<BR>
<EMBED SRC="classical1.mp3">|          ——①

</BODY>

</HTML>
```

② Within the <EMBED> tag, type **WIDTH="?" HEIGHT="?"** replacing ? in both attributes with the width and height values you want to use for the size of the controls.

You can experiment with the values to set just the right size for your page.

```
<HR SIZE="3" NOSHADE>

<CENTER><P><FONT SIZE="4"><B><I>Experts in gardening for over 40 years</I></B></FONT></P>
</CENTER>

<IMG SRC="Million_Bells2.jpg" ALIGN="Left" HSPACE="15">
<IMG SRC="Butterfly3.jpg" ALIGN="Right" HSPACE="15">

<P>We offer the finest selection of plants and planting materials, and an award-winning gardening shop. Stop
by to see our 5 acres of nursery selections, including trees, shrubs, annuals, perennials, and seasonal plants.
Our experienced staff is always available to assist you.</P><BR CLEAR="All">
<BR>

<P>Be sure to visit our store for garden-themed gifts for indoors and outdoors. We feature exciting new items
for home decorating and gardening at the start of each season.</P>

<IMG SRC="Garden_Supplies.jpg" WIDTH="300" HEIGHT="200" ALT="Image of Gardening Tool"
ALIGN="left">   
Music for the Garden<BR>
<EMBED SRC="classical1.mp3" WIDTH="170" HEIGHT="25">     ——②

</BODY>

</HTML>
```

```
<HR SIZE="3" NOSHADE>

<CENTER><P><FONT SIZE="4"><B><I>Experts in gardening for over 40 years</I></B></FONT></P>
</CENTER>

<IMG SRC="Million_Bells2.jpg" ALIGN="Left" HSPACE="15">
<IMG SRC="Butterfly3.jpg" ALIGN="Right" HSPACE="15">

<P>We offer the finest selection of plants and planting materials, and an award-winning gardening shop. Stop
by to see our 5 acres of nursery selections, including trees, shrubs, annuals, perennials, and seasonal plants.
Our experienced staff is always available to assist you.</P><BR CLEAR="All">
<BR>

<P>Be sure to visit our store for garden-themed gifts for indoors and outdoors. We feature exciting new items
for home decorating and gardening at the start of each season.</P>

<IMG SRC="Garden_Supplies.jpg" WIDTH="300" HEIGHT="200" ALT="Image of Gardening Tool"
ALIGN="left">   
Music for the Garden<BR>
<EMBED SRC="classical1.mp3" WIDTH="170" HEIGHT="25" AUTOSTART="false" LOOP="true">


</BODY>

</HTML>
```

- To keep the sound from playing immediately when the page loads, type **AUTOSTART="false"** in the EMBED tag.

- To make the sound play continuously, type **LOOP="true"** in the EMBED tag.

an award-winning gardening shop. Stop by to see our 5 acres of nursery selections, including trees, shrubs, annuals, perennials, and seasonal plants. Our experienced staff is always available to assist you.

Be sure to visit our store for garden-themed gifts for indoors and outdoors. We feature exciting new items for home decorating and gardening at the start of each season.

Music for the Garden

The Web browser displays the sound controls on the page.

- The user can click the **Play** button (▶) to start the sound.

The embedded sound controls act like regular controls for playing, pausing, and stopping the sound.

Note: See Chapter 2 to learn more about viewing your HTML document as an offline Web page.

What audio file formats are common on the Web?

Audio file formats come in several flavors, and some formats are more popular on the Web than others. Here is a list of common audio formats supported by most browsers, plug-ins, and media players:

Audio Formats	
Format	**File Extension**
MP3 (MPEG-1, Layer III)	.mp3
MIDI (Musical Instrument Digital Interface)	.mid
AIFF (Audio Interchange File Format)	.aif
WAV (RIEFF WAVE)	.wav
WMA (Windows Media Audio)	.wma
RA (RealAudio)	.ra

Embed a Video File

You can use the `<EMBED>` tag to add an embedded video clip to your HTML page. Embedded videos play directly on your page. Playback controls also appear on the page allowing the user to start and stop the video.

You can control the size of the video window that appears with an embedded video file. For example, you can set the width at 320 pixels and the height at 240 pixels.

Embed a Video File

1 Type **`<EMBED SRC="?">`** where you want to insert the video window on the page, replacing the ? with the location and name of the video file.

2 Within the `<EMBED>` tag, type **`WIDTH="?" HEIGHT="?"`**, replacing ? in both attributes with the width and height values you want to use for the size of the window.

```
by to see our 5 acres of nursery selections, including trees, shrubs, annuals, perennials, and seasonal plants.
Our experienced staff is always available to assist you.</P><BR CLEAR="All">
<BR>

<P>Be sure to visit our store for garden-themed gifts for indoors and outdoors. We feature exciting new items
for home decorating and gardening at the start of each season.</P>

<IMG SRC="Garden_Supplies.jpg" WIDTH="300" HEIGHT="200" ALT="Image of Gardening Tool"
ALIGN="left">   
Music for the Garden<BR>
<EMBED SRC="classical1.mp3" WIDTH="170" HEIGHT="25" AUTOSTART="false" LOOP="true">
<BR CLEAR="all">
<BR>

<HR SIZE="3" NOSHADE>

<H2>Dealing with Garden Pests</H2>

<P>Is your garden infested? Tired of battling aphids and other pests? You can find plenty of insects that help to
control bad bugs in your garden, and our garden shop can order them for you. For example, did you know that
the Praying Mantis is one of the most useful insects to reside in your garden. Here's an AVI movie clip to show
you more:</P>
<EMBED SRC="Green_Mantis.avi" WIDTH="320" HEIGHT="240" AUTOSTART="true" LOOP="true">

</BODY>

</HTML>
```

Dealing with Garden Pests

Is your garden infested? Tired of battling aphids and other pests? You can find plenty of insects that help to control bad bugs in your garden, and our garden shop can order them for you. For example, did you know that the Praying Mantis is one of the most useful insects to reside in your garden. Here's an AVI movie clip to show you more:

- To make the video play immediately when the page loads, type **AUTOSTART="true"** in the EMBED tag.

  To keep the video from playing immediately when the page loads, type **AUTOSTART="false"** in the EMBED tag.

- To make the video play continuously, type **LOOP="true"** in the EMBED tag.

  The Web browser displays the embedded video window and playback controls on the page.

- The embedded controls act like regular controls for playing, pausing, and stopping the video.

  Note: See Chapter 2 to learn more about viewing your HTML document as an offline Web page.

What video file formats are commonly found on the Web?
Here is a list of common video formats supported by many browsers, plug-ins, and media players:

Audio Formats	
Format	*File Extension*
AVI (Audio/Video Interleaved)	.avi
QT (Apple QuickTime)	.qt
MOV (QuickTime)	.mov
MPG (Motion Picture Experts Group)	.mpg
RV (Real Video)	.rv
DCR (Macromedia Director)	.dcr

Embed a
Flash Movie

You can add a Flash animation to your Web page. Using an ActiveX control number along with the OBJECT element, you can instruct the browser with the necessary information to load and play the Flash file.

Embed a Flash Movie

① Type **<OBJECT CLASSID= "clsid:D27CDB6E-AE6D-11cf-96B8-444553540000"**.

② Type **CODEBASE="http://download. macromedia.com/pub/shockwave/cabs/ flash/swflash.cab#version=6,0,29,0"**.

③ Type **WIDTH="160" HEIGHT="120">**.

④ Type **<PARAM NAME="movie" VALUE="?"/>**, substituting the Flash filename for *?*.

⑤ Type a closing **</OBJECT>**.

● When the user displays your page, the embedded Flash movie plays.

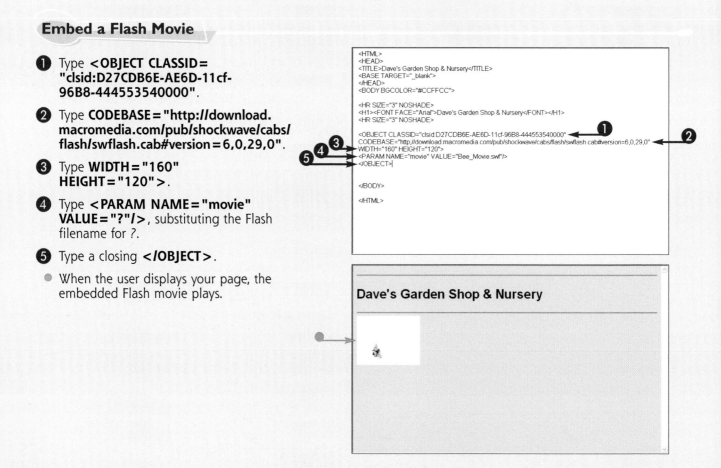

Set Up Background Audio

Because the `<BGSOUND>` element is not part of the HTML standard, you may not want to assign this coding unless you know the majority of your Web page audience uses Internet Explorer as their browser of choice.

You can assign an audio clip to play in the background while users visit your page. Internet Explorer, both Windows and Mac versions, supports a non-standard tag for playing a sound file automatically when a user displays your page.

Set Up Background Audio

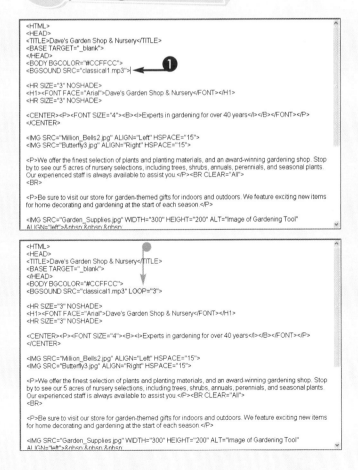

① Type **`<BGSOUND SRC="?">`** on your page, replacing the *?* with the location and name of the audio file.

● To loop the sound to play continuously, type **`LOOP="?"`** within the `<BGSOUND>` tag, replacing *?* with the number of times you want the sound to loop.

You can also set the `LOOP` value to true to make the sound play continuously, **`LOOP="true"`**.

When the user displays your page in Internet Explorer, the background audio plays.

Working with JavaScript

Looking for ways to add action and interest to your Web site? JavaScript can help you add interactivity to your HTML documents. This chapter shows you how to use JavaScripts, through a few examples, to make your pages more interesting to Web site visitors.

Understanding JavaScript

You can use scripts, such as those written in JavaScript, to add dynamic effects to your Web pages. Scripts can turn a static HTML page into an exciting, interactive page that is sure to attract Web visitors. You can use JavaScripts to display message boxes, change images when a user rolls a mouse over an area of the page, validate form information, and much more.

How Scripts Work

Scripts are little programs you can write to add interactivity to Web pages. Scripting instructions can activate when an event occurs, such as when a user clicks something on the page or moves the mouse pointer over an area of the page. Scripts can also activate automatically when the user downloads your page. Because scripts are written in programming languages, you need to know a little bit about programming if you want to write your own scripts. If you want to learn more about writing scripts, visit www.htmlgoodies.com/primers/jsp.

JavaScript

Most Web page scripts are written in the JavaScript language. JavaScript is supported by a vast majority of newer browsers. Originally developed by Netscape, JavaScript is widely used by Web developers to add action and interactivity to Web pages. If you do decide to add scripting to your pages, JavaScript is the best choice. JavaScript is case-sensitive, and requires careful placement of quotes, single quotes, double quotes, and other punctuation, so use care when typing up your scripts.

Client-Side and Server-Side Scripts

Because scripts require a program to read them, you have two options for reading Web page scripts: Web browser or Web server. Scripts read by the Web browser are called *client-side scripts*. Most scripts you use to add action to your Web page are client-side scripts. Scripts read by a Web server are called *server-side scripts*. If your Web site uses forms to collect information from visitors, you commonly use server-side scripts. Server-side scripts work with the server to help databases and other applications collect information from Web pages.

Scripting Tools

You can create your own scripts using an HTML editor. Many editors, such as Macromedia Dreamweaver and Adobe GoLive, offer built-in toolsets to help you create your own scripts without needing to know a lot about programming. You can also easily incorporate scripts that other users have written and add them to your own HTML documents.

Finding Prewritten Scripts

You can find numerous sites on the Internet that offer JavaScripts you can use on your own Web pages. Be sure to ask permission, if needed. For example, sites such as Java-Scripts.net (www.java-scripts.net), JavaScript City (www.javascriptcity.com), and The JavaScript Source (javascript.internet.com), offer free JavaScripts for Web pages.

Scripting Tips

Many users turn off the JavaScript function in their browsers for security reasons. You can use the <NOSCRIPT> and </NOSCRIPT> tags to include alternative text about the script. For example, you might include a simple message like "Your browser does not support this script." It is also good policy to note your scripting language on your HTML document. You can use the <META> tag to identify the type of scripting language you use. The remaining sections of this chapter show you a few JavaScripts you can try out on your own pages.

Understanding Script Events and Handlers

When using JavaScript to add interactivity to your pages, it helps to understand when and why a script executes. Some scripts run as soon as the page downloads, while others require an action on the part of the Web page visitor. As the Web site developer, you decide when and how a script executes. You can use events and event handlers to control your scripts.

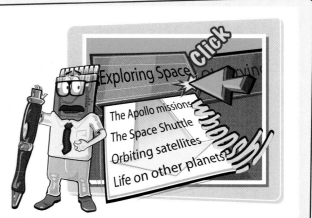

When the user clicks the mouse, the applet launches.

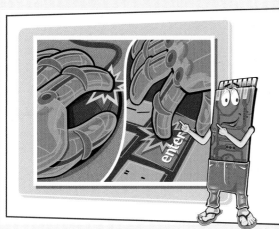

Events

Script *events* are any actions taken by a Web page visitor, such as clicking on an area of the page. The browser can also cause an event, such as loading a page, to occur. For example, mouse events include actions a user performs with a mouse, such as clicking, moving the mouse pointer over an object, or releasing the mouse button after clicking it. Keyboard events include key presses on a keyboard.

Event Handlers

You can determine what happens after an action by specifying an *event handler*. Event handlers associate an object or Web page element with an event. For example, you can use the `onClick` event handler to associate a Web page button with a mouse click. Event handlers are not added using the `<SCRIPT>` tags, but rather, appear within HTML element tags.

Scriptable Events	
Event	*Trigger*
LOAD	Triggers when the page is loaded
UNLOAD	Triggers when the page is unloaded
MOUSEOVER	Triggers when the mouse moves over an object or area on the page
MOUSEOUT	Triggers when the mouse is no longer over an object or area on the page
MOUSEDOWN	Triggers when the mouse is clicked on an object
MOUSEUP	Triggers when the mouse button is released after being clicked
CLICK	Triggers when the user clicks and releases
KEYPRESS	Triggers when a keyboard key is pressed and released
KEYDOWN	Triggers when a keyboard keypress is pressed
KEYUP	Triggers when a keyboard keypress is released
SUBMIT	Triggers when a form button is clicked
RESET	Triggers when a reset form button is clicked

Event Handlers	
Event Handler	*Action*
ONLOAD	A browser loads a page
ONUNLOAD	A browser unloads a page
ONMOUSEOVER	User positions the mouse over an element
ONMOUSEDOWN	User presses the mouse button
ONMOUSEUP	User releases the mouse button
ONMOUSEMOVE	User moves the mouse
ONMOUSEOUT	User moves the mouse away from an element
ONCLICK	User clicks an element
ONDBLCLICK	User double-clicks an element
ONKEYPRESS	User presses and releases a keyboard key
ONKEYDOWN	User presses a key
ONKEYUP	User releases a key
ONSUBMIT	User clicks a Submit button

Add JavaScript to a Web Page

JavaScripts are a great way to add interactivity to your Web pages. You can use the <SCRIPT> and </SCRIPT> tags to add JavaScript to your HTML document. The browser reads anything between the two tags as a script.

To learn more about writing your own JavaScripts, try one of these books: *JavaScript For Dummies, Beginning JavaScript,* or *JavaScript Visual Blueprint*, all from Wiley Publishing, Inc.

Add JavaScript to a Web Page

① Type **<SCRIPT LANGUAGE = "javascript">** where you want to insert the script on the page.

② Type the code for the script you want to add.

In this example, the script tells the user the size of their monitor screen.

③ Type **</SCRIPT>** at the end of the script.

● The Web browser runs the script when the user views your page.

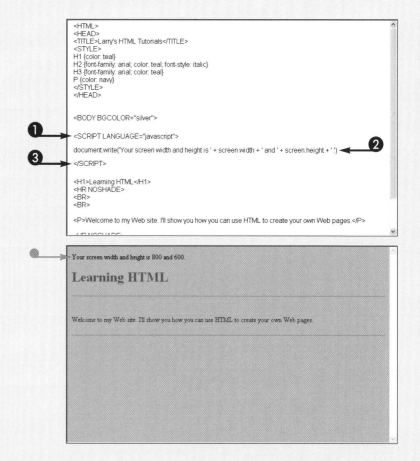

Create a JavaScript File

When you publish your Web pages to a server, be sure to include the linked JavaScript file as part of your file upload. See Chapter 14 to learn more about publishing Web pages.

Many developers prefer to save their scripts in a separate text file and link the file to the Web page. Storing your scripts in a separate file can free up your HTML document to focus just on Web page content. When saving a JavaScript file, use the .js file extension.

Create a JavaScript File

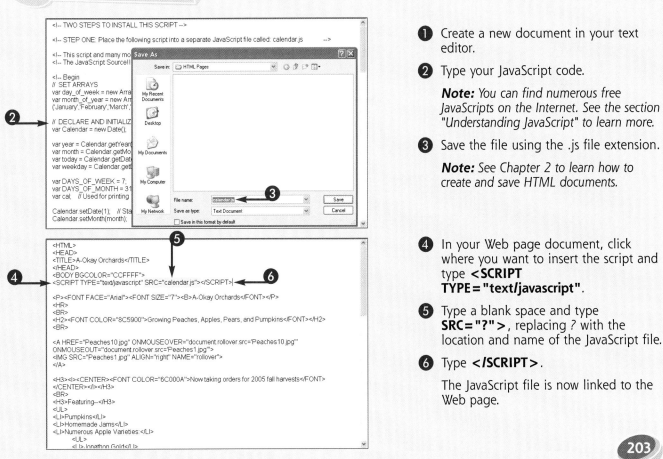

1 Create a new document in your text editor.

2 Type your JavaScript code.

Note: You can find numerous free JavaScripts on the Internet. See the section "Understanding JavaScript" to learn more.

3 Save the file using the .js file extension.

Note: See Chapter 2 to learn how to create and save HTML documents.

4 In your Web page document, click where you want to insert the script and type **<SCRIPT TYPE="text/javascript"**.

5 Type a blank space and type **SRC="?">**, replacing ? with the location and name of the JavaScript file.

6 Type **</SCRIPT>**.

The JavaScript file is now linked to the Web page.

Insert the Current Date and Time

You can use JavaScript to insert the current date and time on your Web page. This can help your page seem current and up-to-date.

Insert the Current Date and Time

① Click where you want to insert the date and time on the page and add a new line.

② Type **<SCRIPT TYPE= "text/javascript">**.

③ Type **document.write(Date())**.

④ Type **</SCRIPT>**.

You may prefer to keep your script on one line, or break it onto multiple lines to make it easier to read.

 The Web browser displays the current date and time.

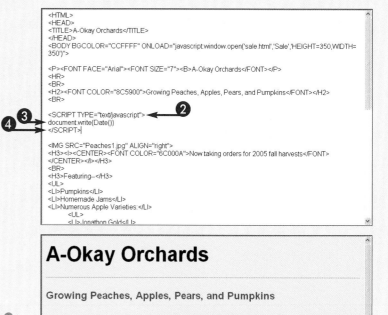

```
<HTML>
<HEAD>
<TITLE>A-Okay Orchards</TITLE>
</HEAD>
<BODY BGCOLOR="CCFFFF" ONLOAD="javascript:window.open('sale.html','Sale',HEIGHT=350,WIDTH=
350')">

<P><FONT FACE="Arial"><FONT SIZE="7"><B>A-Okay Orchards</FONT></P>
<HR>
<BR>
<H2><FONT COLOR="8C5900">Growing Peaches, Apples, Pears, and Pumpkins</FONT></H2>
<BR>

<SCRIPT TYPE="text/javascript">
document.write(Date())
</SCRIPT>

<IMG SRC="Peaches1.jpg" ALIGN="right">
<H3><I><CENTER><FONT COLOR="6C000A">Now taking orders for 2005 fall harvests</FONT>
</CENTER></I></H3>
<BR>
<H3>Featuring--</H3>
<UL>
<LI>Pumpkins</LI>
<LI>Homemade Jams</LI>
<LI>Numerous Apple Varieties:</LI>
    <UL>
        <LI>Jonathon Gold</LI>
```

A-Okay Orchards

Growing Peaches, Apples, Pears, and Pumpkins

Mon Nov 08 12:23:30 2004

Now taking orders for 2005 fall harvests

Featuring--

- **Pumpkins**
- **Homemade Jams**
- **Numerous Apple Varieties:**
    - Jonathon Gold
    - Red Delicious
    - Golden Delicious

Display an Alert Message Box

You can use JavaScript to display an alert message box on your Web page. For example, you might use alert messages to provide special instructions about your site or to alert the user to any important information. After the user reads the message, he or she can close the box.

Display an Alert Message Box

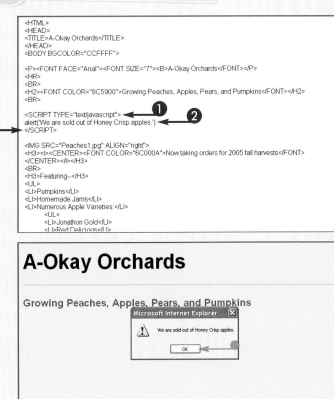

```
<HTML>
<HEAD>
<TITLE>A-Okay Orchards</TITLE>
</HEAD>
<BODY BGCOLOR="CCFFFF">

<P><FONT FACE="Arial"><FONT SIZE="7"><B>A-Okay Orchards</FONT></P>
<HR>
<BR>
<H2><FONT COLOR="8C5900">Growing Peaches, Apples, Pears, and Pumpkins</FONT></H2>
<BR>

<SCRIPT TYPE="text/javascript">
alert('We are sold out of Honey Crisp apples.')
</SCRIPT>

<IMG SRC="Peaches1.jpg" ALIGN="right">
<H3><I><CENTER><FONT COLOR="6C000A">Now taking orders for 2005 fall harvests</FONT>
</CENTER></I></H3>
<BR>
<H3>Featuring--</H3>
<UL>
<LI>Pumpkins</LI>
<LI>Homemade Jams</LI>
<LI>Numerous Apple Varieties:</LI>
    <UL>
    <LI>Jonathon Gold</LI>
    <LI>Red Delicious</LI>
```

A-Okay Orchards

Growing Peaches, Apples, Pears, and Pumpkins

Microsoft Internet Explorer

We are sold out of Honey Crisp apples.

OK

① Type **<SCRIPT TYPE= "text/javascript">**.

② Type **alert('?')**, replacing the *?* with the message text you want to appear in the box.

③ Type **</SCRIPT>** to end the JavaScript code.

The placement of your script on the page determines its order of appearance during the page download.

Place it at the top to load first, or at the bottom to load last.

When the user displays your page in a browser, the alert message box appears.

● The user can click here to close the box.

Display a Pop-Up Window

The pop-up window references a separate HTML file. You will need to create the file before writing the JavaScript. See Chapter 2 to learn more about building HTML documents.

You can use JavaScript to display a pop-up window on your Web page. Pop-up windows are a great way of alerting your Web site visitors to important news about your site, announcing a sale, or describing an upcoming event. The message that appears in the window is actually another Web page created just for the pop-up window.

Display a Pop-Up Window

① Within the <BODY> tag, type **ONLOAD="javascript:window.open('?',**.

Replace ? with the location and name of the Web page you want to appear in the pop-up box.

② Type **'?',** replacing ? with a name for the window.

③ Type **'HEIGHT=?,WIDTH=?')"**, replacing the ? with a height and width size, measured in pixels, for the pop-up window.

When the user displays your page in a browser, the pop-up window appears.

● The user can click here to close the window.

Note: Be very careful about the punctuation you type in a JavaScript. A missed comma or quote can cause an error in your script.

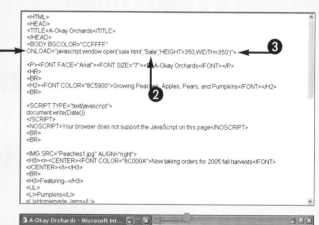

CHAPTER 13

Customize the Status Bar Message for a Link

Ordinarily, when the user moves his or her mouse pointer over a link on your page, the browser's status bar displays the address of the link. You can customize the text that appears in the status bar for a link. For example, you might shorten a complex address to something simpler, or create your own text message to appear instead.

Always be careful about typing single quotes and double quotes in JavaScript code. Do not inadvertently leave any spaces unless the code requires it. A mistype can cause problems with your script.

Customize the Status Bar Message for a Link

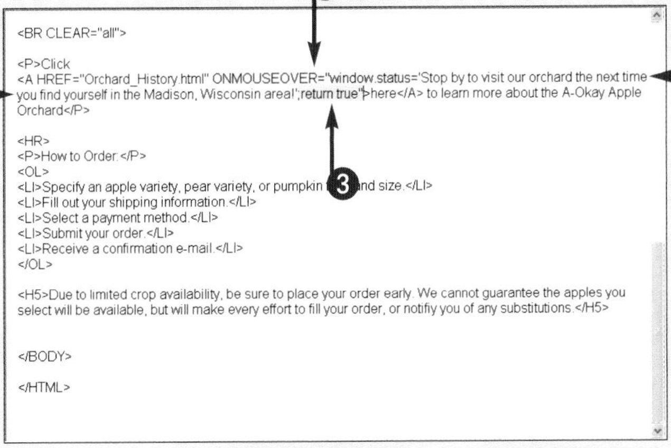

1. Within the <A> tag for the link you want to change, type **ONMOUSEOVER="window.status=**.
2. Type **'** followed by the status bar message text, ending with **'**.

   Anything you type between the single quotes appears in the status bar.
3. Type **;return true"**.

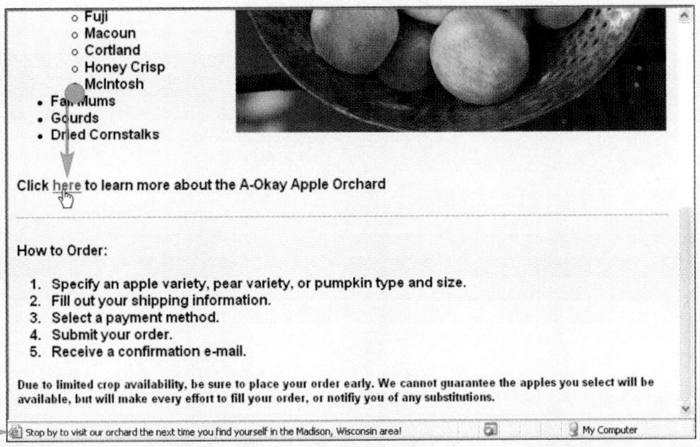

- When the user moves the mouse pointer (↖) over the link, the status bar displays your custom text.

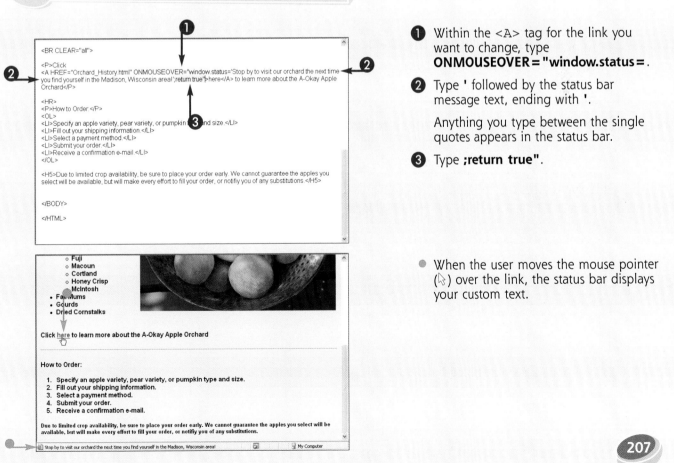

Chapter 14

Publishing Your Web Pages

Are you ready to place your HTML document on the Web? This chapter shows you how to find a Web host and transfer your files to a server.

Understanding Web Page Publishing

The final phase of creating a Web site is publishing your page or pages. In the realm of HTML, the term *publishing* refers to all the necessary steps you must take to make your HTML documents available to others. This includes finding a Web host.

Web Hosts

To place your pages on the Web, you need a Web server — a computer specifically set up to store and manage Web pages. Commonly called *hosts*, Web servers allow you to transfer and store files, including HTML documents, images, and multimedia files. Unless you own your own Web server, you need to find a server to host your pages.

Determine Your Needs

Before you start looking for a Web host, first determine what features and services you need. For example, how much storage space do you anticipate using for your Web site? Does your site require e-commerce features, such as an online shopping cart, or a secure server for handling confidential information? Do you need to keep track of Web statistics, such as who visits your site and how often? Knowing your needs beforehand can help find the right hosting provider.

Web Hosting Scenarios

Numerous companies around the world provide Web site hosting. Some do so for free, in exchange for placing advertising on your site, while others charge a monthly fee. Many ISPs and commercial online services offer their members a certain amount of storage space for free. If you expect your site to generate a lot of traffic, you can use a dedicated Web presence provider — a company that specializes in helping others establish and maintain a presence on the Web. Web presence providers generally offer more features and support.

Search for a Web Host

The best place to start looking for a host is with your own ISP or commercial service. If it does not offer hosting services, you can look for Web hosting services on the Internet. For example, the Web Hosting Ratings site (www.webhostingratings.com/) can help you start your search. Also consider asking friends and family for recommendations, as well as searching through your local yellow pages.

Features to Consider

When considering a Web host, take time to compare what features and services are offered, as well as comparing fees. Find out how much disk space they allow. Although HTML documents are generally small in size, images and multimedia files included with Web pages can consume large amounts of space. Also find out the speed of their connection to the Internet and what advanced features and software they support, such as CGI scripts. Ask whether they offer technical support, register domain names, or provide Web hit statistics to track visitors to your site.

continued

Understanding Web Page Publishing *(continued)*

After you find a host for your Web site and establish a domain name, if needed, the next step to publishing your Web page is to transfer the HTML documents from your computer to the Web server.

Domain Names

Ordinarily, when you publish your pages to a Web host, your Web address is the name of the host's domain followed by the path to your files. If you want a more unique address, you may want to obtain your own domain name. A domain name is a high-level address for a Web site, such as www.wiley.com (owned by the publisher of this book). To acquire a domain name, you must register and pay for the name.

Acquire Your Own Domain Name

You can register for a domain name through VeriSign (www.netsol.com), the keeper of domain names in the United States. Your Web hosting service may also offer a registration service for domain names, for a reduced fee. Once you acquire a domain name, you can ask your Web host to create a virtual domain for your site on their server. This allows you to use your unique domain name rather than the provider's server name in your URL.

Transfer Files

After you set up an account with a Web host, you can transfer your HTML files to the server and set up your Web site. When you transfer files from your computer to a Web server, the activity is called *uploading*. Depending on your server, you can transfer files using FTP (File Transfer Protocol) or a Web interface provided by your hosting service. More often than not, you use FTP to upload your files.

FTP Programs

FTP is the standard for file transfer on the Internet. In order to transfer files with FTP, you need an FTP program, also called a *client*. You can find free and shareware programs on the Internet. Many offer free trials. Popular FTP programs include WS_FTP for Windows (www.ipswitch.com/ Products/WS_FTP/), CuteFTP (www.globalscape. com/products/cuteFTP), and Fetch for Mac (www.dartmouth.edu/pages/sofdev/fetch.html). You should also check your Web host to see what FTP clients or file upload tools they may offer. See the section, "Transfer Files to a Web Server with WS_FTP" for more information.

Maintain Your Site

After you upload your pages, you can view and test your site. One of your chores as a Web developer is to maintain your Web site. It is up to you to keep your information and links current. It is good practice to regularly test your site for broken links. Although some sites need more updating than others, it is also good practice to update your content on a regular basis or give it a fresh look or tweak from time to time. Stale data can keep visitors from returning to your site.

Publicize Your Site

Once you have published your Web site, you can look for ways to attract visitors. You can use keywords and useful page titles to gain the attention of search engines. You can also advertise your pages on other sites, through e-mails, and offline.

Transfer Files to a Web Server with WS_FTP

You can transfer your Web page files to a Web server using FTP software. In this section, you learn how to transfer files using Ipswitch WS_FTP, a program designed specially for transferring files on the Web. If you use another FTP program, your steps may differ.

Transfer Files to a Web Server with WS_FTP

SET UP YOUR CONNECTION

1 Open the WS_FTP program window.

The first time you use the program, the Connection Wizard appears to help you set up your server connection.

Note: *If you have not downloaded and installed the program, visit www.ipswitch.com.*

2 Type in a name for your server or Web site.

3 Click **Next**.

4 Type in your server address.

If you do not know the server address, contact your Web host for more information.

Typically, you receive this information when you sign up for an account.

5 Click **Next**.

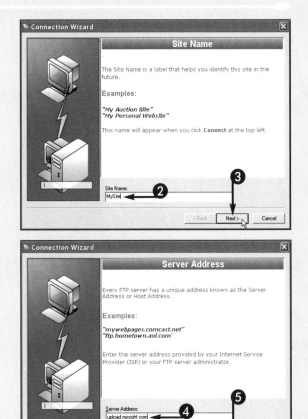

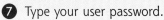

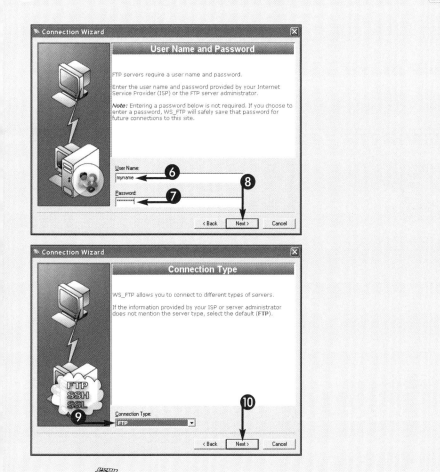

6 Type your user name.

7 Type your user password.

If you do not know your user ID or password, contact your Web host.

Typically, you receive this information when you sign up for an account.

8 Click **Next**.

9 Select a connection type, if needed.

FTP is the default selection.

10 Click **Next**.

Where can I find an FTP program?
You can find numerous FTP programs on the Internet, including freeware and shareware programs. Many programs offer a free trial version you can experiment with to see if you want to purchase the program. You can find a trial version of Ipswitch WS_FTP at www.ipswitch.com.

What information do I need to set up an account with an FTP program?
Most servers ask you for a server address, a user name, and a password. When you create an account with a Web host provider, you are assigned this information, including a destination folder on the server's directory. You can use this folder to store your HTML files, along with any image and multimedia files you include with your Web page. Be sure to contact your Web host for this information before attempting to upload files for the first time.

Transfer Files to a Web Server with WS_FTP *(continued)*

You can upload a single file or multiple files. Any time you need to update your site, you can transfer more files to the server.

After you establish your server connection, you can start transferring files. The WS_FTP program window shows two panes, one displaying the files on your computer, and the other for displaying files on your server. You can move files between the two using the Upload and Download buttons.

Transfer Files to a Web Server with WS_FTP *(continued)*

● You can click this option if you immediately want to open your connection once you complete the Connection Wizard.

⑪ Click **Finish**.

Your connection information is saved and the program window remains open and ready for any file transfer activities you want to perform.

TRANSFER FILES

① If you have not connected to your server, click the **Connect** button ().

Note: *You must connect to the Internet before transferring files.*

② Click your connection name from the list.

WS_FTP connects your computer to the server.

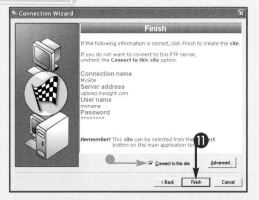

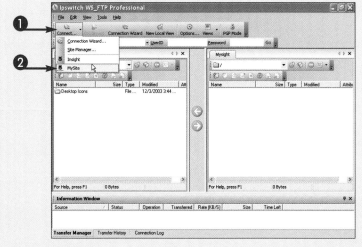

③ Click the files you want to transfer.

To select multiple files, press and hold **Shift** while clicking filenames.

④ Click the **Upload** button (■).

WS_FTP transfers the files.

Depending on the file size, the transfer may take several minutes.

● The transferred files appear listed on the server.

⑤ Click the **Close** button (⊠) to exit the program when you have finished transferring files.

You can now use your browser to view the pages.

How do I remove a file from my Web site?

Open your connection to the server, select the file you want to delete from the left pane and press the Delete button (📖). A prompt box appears asking if you really want to remove the file. Click **Yes** to immediately remove your file from the server.

Can I transfer a new version of the same file already found on the server?

Yes. You can overwrite existing files. WS_FTP prompts you if the same file is found on the server. You then have the option of overwriting the file with the new file. Simply click **Overwrite** in the prompt box. If you prefer to wait and check the file later, click **Skip** and WS_FTP leaves the original file on the server intact.

Index

Index

Index

Index

scripts
    client-side versus server-side, 199
    prewritten, 199
    as term, 198
ScriptSearch, 166
scroll bars, 173
search engine keywords, 17, 29
<SELECT NAME SIZE>, 178–179
SELECTED value, 179
selector, style sheet, 62, 63
semicolon (;), 11, 63
server-side script, 199
shading, 59
silver color, 55
simple text editors, 9
single quotes, 207
size
    font, 52–53
    image, 101–103
    of sound controls, 190
    table, 131, 144–145
    of text box, 170
    of video controls, 192
SIZE attribute, 53, 59
slash (/), 10, 11
small a, grave accent (à), 45
small a, tilde (ã), 45
small n, tilde (ñ), 45
small o, slash (ø), 45
soft wrap, 173
SOLID border value, 90
source code
    copying, 13
    printing, 13
    saving, 13
    viewing, 12, 29
space
    around image, 111
    blank, 35
spacing, line. *See* line spacing
<SPAN>, 73
spanning cells, 124
special characters, 44–45
speeds, connection, 4
standards, HTML, 6
START attribute, 41
status bar message, 207
streaming media files, 185
strict version HTML, 16, 26, 27
<STYLE>, 68–69
style sheet text formatting
    alignment, 85
    bold, 78
    border, 90–91
    case, 84
    changing fonts, 82–83
    color, 89
    font size, 81
    indent, 80
    italics, 79
    line spacing control, 86
    margins, 87
    padding, 88
    position control, 92–93
    vertical alignment, 95
    wrap text, 94
style sheets, 62–75
    borders with, 133
    class in, 70–71
    comments on, 67

controlling multiple pages with, 62
defining, 62
<DIV> on, 72–73
external, 64–65
in HTML version 4, 7
ID attribute, 75
internal, 68–69
linking to, 66
local application, 74
multiple, 65
saving, 65
syntax of, 62–63
SUBJECT attribute, 125
submenus, 179
submit button, 162, 165, 180
SUBMIT event handler, 201
superscript one (¹), 45
superscript two (²), 45
superscript three (³), 45
surfing, Web, 5
syntax
    HTML, 10–11
    style sheet, 62–63

T

<TABLE>, 129–131
<TABLE BORDER>, 132, 142–143
<TABLE BORDERCOLOR>, 132, 133
<TABLE CAPTION>, 141
<TABLE CELLPADDING>, 134
<TABLE CELLSPACING>, 135
table data, 129, 130
table header, 130, 138, 140
<TABLE HEIGHT>, 144–145
table row, 129, 130
<TABLE WIDTH>, 144–145
tables
    adding, 130–131
    border display controls, 142–143
    borders on, 132–133
    building, 131
    captions, 141
    cell padding/spacing, 134–135
    cell width/height, 136–137
    column labels, 138
    elements of, 125
    headers, 140
    newspaper-style columns, 139
    preparing for, 125
    presentation, 125
    size, 131, 144–145
    span cells across columns/rows, 146–147
    structure of, 128–129
    traditional, 125
tag pairs, 10
tags
    definition of, 10
    entering, 19
    opening/closing, 6, 10
    in XHTML, 7
TARGET attribute, 120–121, 158–159
TCP/IP (Transmission Control Protocol/Internet Control), 5
<TD> (table detail), 129, 130
<TD COLSPAN>, 146
<TD HEIGHT>, 137
<TD ROWSPAN>, 147
<TD VALIGN>, 139
<TD WIDTH>, 136
teal color, 55

224

If this book helped you, check out these other Simplified® titles.

All designed for visual learners—just like you!

0-7645-8329-8

0-7645-9752-3

0-7645-9999-2

Visual®
An Imprint of **WILEY**
Now you know.